Series / Number 07-018

ANALYZING PANEL DATA

GREGORY B. MARKUS
University of Michigan

SAGE PUBLICATIONS / Beverly Hills / London

For information address:

SAGE Publications, Inc.
275 South Beverly Drive
Beverly Hills, California 90212

SAGE Publications Ltd
28 Banner Street
London EC1Y 8QE, England

International Standard Book Number 0-8039-1372-9

Library of Congress Catalog Card No. L.C. 79-91899

SIXTH PRINTING, 1988

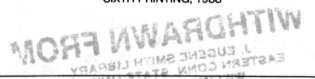

When citing a professional paper, please use the proper form. Remember to cite the correct
Sage University Paper series title and include the paper number. One of the two following
formats can be adapted (depending on the style manual used):

(1) IVERSEN, GUDMUND R. and NORPOTH, HELMUT (1976) "Analysis of Variance." Sage University Paper series on Quantitative Applications in the Social Sciences, 07-001. Beverly Hills and London: Sage Pubns.

OR

(2) Iversen, Gudmund R. and Norpoth, Helmut. 1976. *Analysis of Variance*. Sage University Paper series on Quantitative Applications in the Social Sciences, series no. 07-001. Beverly Hills and London: Sage Publications.

CONTENTS

Editor's Introduction

In ANALYZING PANEL DATA, Gregory B. Markus presents a broad introduction to various statistical techniques available for the analysis of panel data. In an earlier paper in this series, TIME SERIES ANALYSIS, Charles W. Ostrom, Jr., presented a discussion of techniques appropriate to the analysis of observations taken on a *single* case at a relatively *large* number of time points. In this paper, Markus discusses techniques appropriate to the analysis of observations taken on *many* cases—at a relatively *few* number of time points (usually less than five). He presents a lucid introduction to techniques for the analysis of panel data, including both discrete and continuous variables, and he uses a large number of simple examples to clarify more difficult points.

Professor Markus discusses—in his paper's first half—the use of numerous *techniques appropriate to the analysis of discrete or categorical data*. He begins with a discussion of Markov models, which are used to provide representations of dynamic processes. Unfortunately, Markov models have two shortcomings: They do not incorporate measurement error, and they do not explain change over time—they merely describe that change. Markus then moves to a discussion of models suggested by L. M. Wiggins and J. S. Coleman, which incorporate measurement error into the analysis. He ends the discussion of discrete variables by presenting a discussion of L. Goodman's log-linear models and the use of regression analysis on dichotomous dependent variables, which allows the researcher to examine simultaneously a larger set of variables.

The second half of this paper discusses the *analysis of continuous variables* in panel analysis. Markus provides an excellent discussion of regression effects, autocorrelation, and measurement error . . . all serious problems in the analysis of panel data. He introduces techniques proposed by D. Heise, by Wiley and Wiley, and by Joreskog for the analysis of panel data. All of these techniques are based on causal modeling and regression analysis, so an understanding of those topics is necessary for a full comprehension of the latter half of this paper.

Professor Markus not only presents a lucid summary and introduction to the techniques mentioned above but he also provides helpful discussions of the advantages and disadvantages of each of these techniques. He makes ample use of examples, to illustrate appropriate and inappropriate uses of each technique. The beginning student should be able to follow this presentation without much difficulty and, once finished with it, should have a very good sense of how to deal appropriately with most problems confronting researchers dealing with panel data.

ANALYZING PANEL DATA is a useful starting place for researchers
in many different fields, including (among others):

- psychologists who conduct longitudinal analyses for the study of
  child as well as adult socialization processes
- sociologists who study aging by examining the same set of individuals
  through part of the life cycle
- political scientists who study public opinion and voting by the use
  of panel surveys
- sociologists and polotical scientists who study aggregation—nations,
  states, organizations, and so on—by studying sets of such aggre-
  gations over relatively few time points.

There are, of course, many other disciplines and many other sets of problems which can use the techniques outlined in this paper on panel data.
Most readers should find this introduction to the topic not only relevant
to their research problems but also easy to read and a first-rate example
of methodological pedagogy.

—John L. Sullivan, Series Editor

ANALYZING PANEL DATA

GREGORY B. MARKUS
University of Michigan

1. INTRODUCTION

The purpose of this paper is to introduce the reader to a variety of techniques which are useful for analyzing data from a *panel study*. Panel data are typically thought of as information obtained by interviewing a sample of respondents—a panel—at two or more points in time. And, indeed, many panel data are of this type. But there are data other than of the survey kind that may be thought of as arising from a panel study. For instance, aggregate indicators collected on many countries but at relatively few time points, e.g., the *World Handbook* data (Taylor and Hudson, 1972), may be treated as data on a panel of nations. Information from an experiment in which subjects are repeatedly observed may be similarly regarded as panel data.

The principal difference between a time series and panel data is that, with respect to the former, observations are usually taken on a single entity (individual, country, corporation, and such) at a relatively large number of time points, while in the latter the observations are on many entities but at relatively few times—almost always four or less. In time series analysis, the time point is the unit of analysis (Ostrom, 1978), while for panel analysis it is the individual. This distinction should not be overemphasized, however, since there are instances in which it is useful to conceive of panel data as a pooling of a large number of short time series

AUTHOR'S NOTE: *Much of this paper was written while the author was a Guest Professor at the Zentralarchiv fuer Umfragen, Methoden, and Analyzen at the University of Mannheim. The support provided by ZUMA is gratefully acknowledged. Thanks are also extended to Philip E. Converse and Lutz Erbring for their comments on an earlier draft. All data used in this paper are available from the Inter-university Consortium for Political and Social Research.*

(one for each individual). Furthermore, many analytical issues, such as the problems posed by serially dependent disturbances, are common to research utilizing either kind of data.

For that matter, the separation of panel analysis from the analysis of multiple cross-sections (in which the sample is drawn anew each time) is also to some extent artificial. Many of the analytical techniques to be discussed here may be applied to cross-sectional as well as longitudinal data, with some modifications.

The focus of this paper is *analysis*, as opposed to problems of panel sampling or design. The latter issues—panel mortality, contamination through repeated measurement, the changing meanings of instrument items, and so on—are clearly of concern to the panel data analyst, but they are largely ignored here. The reader is referred to Campbell and Stanley (1963), Kish (1965), and Hyman (1972) for an introduction. The emphasis here is also on *application* rather than theory. Nevertheless, it is important for the practicing researcher to see that particular analytical techniques do not "drop out of the sky" but are derived logically from a set of basic assumptions. As much as is possible in a brief presentation, I have endeavored to provide an intuitive grasp of this logic without going into the finer details of statistical theory.

The first section of this paper is devoted to the analysis of discrete variables, either dichotomies or polytomies. The second section extends the discussion to continuous (or, more strictly, interval level) variables. This extension assumes a familiarity with multiple regression analysis; the reader who requires an introduction or review of multiple regression should refer to any standard introductory econometrics text, such as Johnston (1972), Kmenta (1971), or Hanushek and Jackson (1977).

2. ANALYSIS OF DISCRETE VARIABLES

Markov Models

A number of researchers have suggested the utility of a class of probability models termed *Markov chains* for the analysis of panel data (Anderson, 1954; Goodman, 1962; Kemeny et al., 1966). In its simplest form, a Markov chain represents a change process that occurs in discrete time and with reference to a discrete state variable, such as vote intention or occupational classification. A *first-order* Markov chain is one in which the probability of an individual being in a particular state of the variable of interest at time $t + 1$ is solely a function of his location at time t. The vector P of probabilities that the individual is in state i, $i = 1, 2, \ldots, s$, at time t, plus the s × s matrix of transition probabilities, R, completely describe the process (see Table 1). Typically, the parameters of a first-order Markov process are estimated from the marginal proportions of individuals in states i at time t and from the contingency table of observed change from times t to t + 1.

As an empirical example, Table 2, which is derived from the Butler and Stokes (1969) study of political change in Britain, shows how respondents identified themselves as middle or working class in 1963 and 1964. The estimated transition probabilities are derived by transforming the cell frequencies into row proportions, yielding:

$$R = \begin{bmatrix} .76 & .24 \\ .13 & .87 \end{bmatrix}.$$

The R matrix indicates that if an individual saw himself as belonging to the middle class at time t, the probability is .76 that he will give the same response at t + 1. Similarly, the probability of stable working class identification is .87. The complements of these values are the probabilities of switching from middle to working class identification, and vice versa.

Given these data—and assuming the process is first-order Markovian—one may predict the proportion of middle and working class identifiers at t = 3. The marginal class proportions at t = 2 (i.e., 1964) are, from Table 2,

$$P = [.29 \quad .71].$$

Hence one would predict that:

.29	proportion middle class at t = 2
× .76	probability of stable middle-class response
.2204	stable middle-class responses at t = 3
.71	proportion working class at t = 2
× .13	probability of switching to middle-class response
.0923	switches to middle class at t = 3.

In sum, the expectation is that about 22% + 9% = 31% of respondents at t = 3 will locate themselves in the middle class. The remaining 69% will

TABLE 1
Parameters of a First-Order Markov Chain

State at time t + 1

$$\begin{array}{c} \text{State at} \\ \text{time t} \end{array} \quad \begin{array}{c} 1 \\ 2 \\ \vdots \\ s \end{array} \begin{bmatrix} r_{11} & r_{12} & \cdots & r_{1s} \\ r_{21} & r_{22} & \cdots & r_{2s} \\ \vdots & \vdots & & \cdot \\ r_{s1} & r_{s2} & \cdots & r_{ss} \end{bmatrix} = R \qquad \sum_{j=1}^{s} r_{ij} = 1.0, \quad i = 1, 2, \ldots, s$$

$$\begin{array}{c} \text{Probability of} \\ \text{state i at} \end{array} \begin{bmatrix} p_1 & p_2 & \cdots & p_s \end{bmatrix} = P \qquad \sum_{i=1}^{s} p_i = 1.0$$

TABLE 2
British Social Class Identification, 1963-1964

		1964		
		Middle	Working	Total
1963	Middle	198	64	262
	Working	94	639	733
		292	703	995

be working class at t = 3. These same results may be obtained directly by matrix multiplication:[1]

$$PR = \begin{bmatrix} .29 & .71 \end{bmatrix} \begin{bmatrix} .76 & .24 \\ .13 & .87 \end{bmatrix} = \begin{bmatrix} .31 & .69 \end{bmatrix}.$$

If the panel study contains more than two waves, the goodness of fit of the Markov model may be evaluated by comparing predictions with observed results or by comparing transition matrices based on successive pairs of waves. With regard to the British panel, the prediction of 31% middle class is quite close to the observed fraction of 29% for the third wave (1966).[2] This fit may be evaluated more precisely by testing the hypothesis that the transition matrix of change from t = 1 to t = 2 is equal to the matrix based on the t = 2 and t = 3 data. Following Goodman (1962), we shall employ the usual chi-square test applied to contingency tables. The data on observed change from 1964 to 1966 are shown in Table 3.

The usual chi-square statistic (Hays, 1973) is calculated for each section of Table 4, and the two chi-square values are summed. Each 2 x 2 section has one degree of freedom, so for the sum of the two chi-squares, df = 2. The calculated results for Table 4 are $\chi^2 = 2.01$ for the middle-class section and $\chi^2 = .57$ for the working class section. Consulting a tabulation of chi-square values, one finds that neither value approaches significance ($\alpha > .10$), nor does their sum. The hypothesis of a constant transition matrix appears to be a reasonable one.

STEADY STATE

If a change process is described by a constant transition matrix, and if the process is allowed to run for a large number of time periods, an equilibrium or steady state will eventually be reached. The steady state is one in which the proportions or probabilities in the P vector no longer change from one period to the next. With reference to our social class example, the steady state occurs when the marginal proportions of working class and middle-class identifiers are stable. Individuals may continue to alter their responses over time in the steady state, but the aggregate proportions remain constant.

Suppose for purposes of exposition that the process of class identification began with no respondents in the middle class at t = 0. The expected fractions for t = 1 would be found as follows:

$$[0.00 \quad 1.00] \begin{bmatrix} .76 & .24 \\ .13 & .87 \end{bmatrix} = [.13 \quad .87].$$

Thus, at t = 1, about 13% of the sample should be middle-class identifiers. Similarly, at t = 2 one would expect about 21% of respondents to locate themselves in the middle class, since:

$$[.13 \quad .87] \begin{bmatrix} .76 & .24 \\ .13 & .87 \end{bmatrix} = [.21 \quad .79].$$

The results obtained by continuing these calculations are graphed in Figure 1. It is clear from the graph that the fraction of middle-class identi-

TABLE 3
British Social Class Identification, 1964-1966

| | | 1966 | | |
		Middle	Working	Total
1964	Middle	.70 (205)	.30 (87)	1.00 (292)
	Working	.12 (81)	.88 (622)	1.00 (703)
		.29 (286)	.71 (709)	1.00 (995)

TABLE 4
Turnover Data for Test of Equal Transition Matrices

| | | Response at t + 1 | | |
		Middle	Working	Total
Middle class at t	t = 1 (1963)	198	64	262
	t = 2 (1964)	205	87	292
		403	151	554

| | | Response at t + 1 | | |
		Middle	Working	Total
Working class at t	t = 1 (1963)	94	639	733
	t = 2 (1964)	81	622	703
		175	1261	1436

fiers is converging on a steady state value. How is this value estimated? If one lets the unknown equilibrium proportions be p_1 and p_2, then by definition of the steady state one may set up the following equality:

$$[p_1 \quad p_2] \begin{bmatrix} .76 & .24 \\ .13 & .87 \end{bmatrix} = [p_1 \quad p_2].$$

In scalar algebra, we have the equations:

$$.76 \; p_1 + .13 \; p_2 = p_1$$

$$.24 \; p_1 + .87 \; p_2 = p_2$$

and, by definition, $p_1 + p_2 = 1.00$.

When these equations are solved for the unknowns, we find that the system is predicted to "settle down" to a mix of about 35% middle-class and 65% working class identifiers. For an interesting application of equilibrium prediction to the study of political partisanship, see Converse (1969).

We have found evidence suggesting that a first-order Markov chain fits the British data on changing class identification rather well. It is not unusual, however, for observations to depart significantly from expectations based on such a simple model of change. In such cases, either of two modifications of the simple Markov model may be appropriate. They are: (1) increasing the order of the Markov process and (2) developing a model with varying transition matrices across substrata of the sample.

SECOND-ORDER PROCESS

As in the Butler-Stokes research, a question dealing with social class identification was also posed to respondents in the 1956-58-60 American National Election Panel Study conducted by the Survey Research Center at the University of Michigan. Examination of the transition matrices for these data indicates a significant difference between class identification turnover in 1956-1958 and 1958-1960. This result might suggest that the change process is not Markovian, that a Markov process is appropriate but that different transition rates apply to different substrata of the sample, or any of a number of other hypotheses. For illustrative purposes, we shall consider the possibility that the change process is *second-order* rather than first-order Markovian.

A second-order Markov chain is one in which the states occupied by an individual at times $t - 2$ and $t - 1$ jointly determine the probabilities of transition between $t - 1$ and t. Table 5 displays the observed second-order transition matrix for the 1956-58-60 American panel.

It is apparent from Table 5 that transition probabilities linking class identifications in 1958 and 1960 vary with 1956 identification. For example, the probability of stable middle-class identification between 1958 and 1960 is .76 if the respondent was also middle class in 1956, but it is only .43 if the 1956 identification was with the working class.

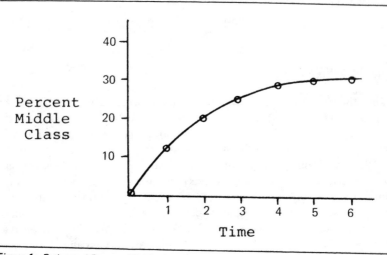

Figure 1: Estimated Percent Middle Class Based on Constant Transition

TABLE 5
American Social Class Identification Transition, 1956-1958-1960

1956	1958	1960		
		Middle	Working	Total
M	M	.76 (216)	.24 (70)	1.00 (286)
W	M	.43 (56)	.57 (75)	1.00 (131)
M	W	.31 (42)	.69 (92)	1.00 (134)
W	W	.08 (47)	.92 (549)	1.00 (596)
		.31 (361)	.69 (786)	1.00 (1147)

Goodman (1962) has suggested that a chi-square test be employed to test the hypothesis that the transition process is second order rather than first order. The procedure is quite similar to the test applied to Table 4. One first divides Table 5 along the dashed line to form two subtables. Chi-square values are calculated for the subtables and then summed. The results are $\chi^2 = 42.6$ (df = 1) and 56.2 (df = 1) for the subtables, and $\chi^2 = 98.2$ (df = 2) for the complete table. These chi-square values are far in excess of any reasonable significance level, leading to a rejection of the null hypothesis of a first-order chain in favor of the hypothesis of a second-order process.

In a manner that parallels the method used with first-order models, a second-order model can be used to generate predictions for t + 1, t + 2, and so on (Goodman, 1962). Ideally, one would prefer to possess additional waves of data to test the goodness of fit of these predictions. Additional waves would also permit a chi-square test of whether the process was of an order higher than second. Unfortunately, only three waves of data are available for the panel study used in the example. In principle, higher order Markov processes are possible; e.g., a third-order process would be one in which the states occupied at times t – 3, t – 2, and t – 1 jointly determine the response state at time t. In practice, however, social science applications of processes beyond second order are rare.

MARKOV MODELS FOR HETEROGENEOUS POPULATIONS

A second approach to situations for which a first-order Markov chain does not fit is to subdivide the sample into strata, each with its own distinct set of transition probabilities. In the simplest version of this strategy, the sample is stratified along the values of some new variable introduced into the analysis. Whether or not it makes sense in a given research problem to allow for heterogeneous transition rates, to increase the order of the Markov process, or both is ultimately a substantive issue rather than a purely statistical one. Statistical analysis can indicate whether a particular model is consistent with the data at hand. But the initial decision to evaluate one model out of the many possible models is based primarily on the researcher's substantive knowledge concerning the problem under study.

As Coleman (1964b) has noted, the incorporation of independent stratifying variables into the analysis increases one's understanding of the process. The problem, of course, is finding stratifying variables which significantly decrease within-strata and increase between-strata heterogeneity of transition rates. With reference to the American panel data, one factor which might plausibly affect transition rates for class identification is whether respondents perceived their financial situation to have improved or worsened in the time between waves. The expectation is that the probability of working class identification at time t should be relatively higher for respondents who felt that their financial status declined, identification at t – 1 held constant. As Table 6 shows, this is the case.

TABLE 6

Transition Rates for Class Identification, by Perceived Change
in Financial Status, 1956-1958

| | | Better Financial Change 1958 | | |
		Middle	Working	Total
	Middle	.80	.20	1.00
		(93)	(23)	(116)
1956				
	Working	.21	.79	1.00
		(26)	(95)	(121)
		.50	.50	1.00
		(119)	(118)	(237)

| | | Worse Financial Change 1958 | | |
		Middle	Working	Total
	Middle	.56	.44	1.00
		(28)	(22)	(50)
1956				
	Working	.10	.90	1.00
		(7)	(66)	(73)
		.28	.72	1.00
		(35)	(88)	(123)

Once again, a chi-square test may be employed to determine whether
the two transition matrices in Table 6 are significantly different from
each other. Comparing the two middle-class rows, χ^2 (df = 1) = 10.33,
$\alpha < .01$; and for the two working class rows, χ^2 (df = 1) = 4.57, $\alpha < .05$. The
summed χ^2 value is 14.90, $\alpha < .01$. Thus, the stratification of the sample by
perceived financial change has resulted in significantly different transition
matrices. Moreover, when a table comparable to Table 6 is constructed
for the 1958-60 data (not shown), the results are quite similar. A chi-
square test indicates that, within each strata, the transition matrix is
essentially constant over time.

MOVER-STAYER MODEL

Blumen et al. (1955) applied a different approach to heterogeneous
transition rates in a study of labor mobility. This model, termed the
"mover-stayer" model, does not employ independent variables to stratify

the sample, but instead is based on the a priori assumption that the population may be divided into two subgroups, one which is perfectly stable from one time to the next and one for which movement from state to state is Markovian (see also, Goodman, 1961).

A special case of the mover-stayer model occurs when the behavior of the movers is assumed to the random, i.e., all states are equiprobable regardless of prior state. Converse (1964, 1970) found that change in certain political attitudes was consistent with this "black-white" model. That is, it appeared that respondents could be divided into those having perfectly stable attitudes on an issue and those who possessed no real opinions on the matter and, hence, responded randomly over time.

The logic of the mover-stayer approach may be illustrated with the American panel data. The 1956-1958 class identification turnover table (Table 7) displays features which suggest that the Converse black-white model might be a reasonable representation of the underlying change process: The marginals are virtually identical for the two waves, as are the frequencies in the off-diagonal "mover" cells. This is the pattern that one would expect if the only change occurring was within a subgroup of respondents who circulated randomly between categories from one time point to the next.

For the movers, the four possible transition patterns (M-M, M-W, W-M, W-W) are equally likely, just as "heads-heads," "heads-tails," and so on are equally likely sequences for successive tosses of a fair coin. Therefore, given the 134 observed movers in the M-W cell, there is assumed to be an equal number of M-M respondents who are movers who happened to give the response of "middle class" at $t = 1$ and $t = 2$. Similarly, 131 of the W-W individuals are assumed to be movers, to match the 131 W-M movers. Based on these assumptions, the observed frequencies in Table 7 are decomposed as shown in Table 8.

The accuracy of the black-white model may be gauged by comparing predictions derived from it with observed behavior. Consider first the *observed* movers in Table 7. Since their transition probabilities are assumed to equal .5, we would expect their 1958-60 turnover table to be as shown in Table 9A. The expected turnover of the *observed* stayers is a bit more complicated but follows directly from the black-white model. As shown in Table 8, the 286 M-M respondents are assumed to consist of 152 true stayers plus 134 movers, who respond randomly. We would expect half of the 134 movers to switch to a working class response in 1960. Similarly, half of the 131 movers in the W-W cell should call themselves middle class in 1960, leading to the predictions for the 1956-58 observed stayers that are displayed in Table 9B.

TABLE 7
Social Class Identification Transition in the United States, 1956-1958

		1958		
		Middle	Working	Total
1956	Middle	286	134	420
	Working	131	596	727
		417	730	1147

TABLE 8
Decomposition of Change in Social Class Identification

		Movers					Stayers						
		1958					1958					1958	
		M	W				M	W				M	W
	M	134	134			M	152	0			M	286	134
1956				+	1956				=	1956			
	W	131	131			W	0	465			W	131	596

It is now a simple matter of comparing these predictions with the observed 1958-1960 turnover tables and calculating the four chi-square values. The observed transitions and the results of the tests are shown in Table 10. The chi-square tests indicate that the black-white model fits fairly well for the 1956-1958 observed stayers and for the W-M movers. Significantly more M-W movers remained in the working class category in 1960 than was predicted by the model, however, leading to a rejection of the black-white model.

SOME LIMITATIONS OF MARKOV MODELS

It should be clear from the discussion that Markov models are useful for a variety of analytical tasks. There are, nevertheless, some short-comings of these models that should be taken into account. First, and perhaps most important, although simple Markov chains may provide useful representations of dynamic processes, they do not explain *why* individuals change over time. They simply describe the probabilities associated with transitions from one state to another. Stratification of

TABLE 9

**Expected 1958-1960 Turnover for Observed 1956-1958
Movers and Stayers**

A. Observed Movers

		1960		
		M	W	Total
1958	M	65.5	65.5	131
	W	67	67	134
		132.5	132.5	265

B. Observed Stayers

		1960		
		M	W	Total
1958	M	219	67	286
	W	65.5	530.5	596
		284.5	597.5	882

the sample by levels of an independent variable may yield some explanatory power, but the procedure is cumbersome when more than one or two additional variables are introduced into the analysis.

The Markov approach is also limited by its general inability to deal with measurement error. With the exception of certain models, such as the black-white model, simple Markov models assume that all observed change is true change; but when the variables of interest are survey responses or other fallible measures, observed change will almost certainly contain some unreliability. Social scientists working with Markov models have been particularly troubled by this problem. We turn next to two modifications of the Markov scheme which attempt to separate true change from error.

Wiggins Models

Wiggins (1973) extended the application of Markov models to panel data in two ways. First, Markovian change was only one of a variety of

TABLE 10
Test of the Black-White Model of Social Class Identification

Middle class "stayers"

| | 1960 | |
	M	W
Predicted	219	67
Observed	216	70

$\chi^2 = .09, \quad \alpha > .50$

Working class "stayers"

| | 1960 | |
	M	W
Predicted	65.5	530.5
Observed	47	549

$\chi^2 = 3.36, \quad \alpha > .05$

W-M "movers"

| | 1960 | |
	M	W
Predicted	65.5	65.5
Observed	56	75

$\chi^2 = 1.39, \quad \alpha > .25$

M-W "movers"

| | 1960 | |
	M	W
Predicted	67	67
Observed	42	92

$\chi^2 = 9.67, \quad \alpha < .005$

Total χ^2 (d.f. = 4) = 14.51, $\quad \alpha < .01$

change processes permitted by his approach. Second, the Wiggins models explicitly incorporate the idea that an individual's manifest response to a survey item is but an imperfect reflection of an unobservable underlying attitude, or latent attitude in Wiggins's terminology. For example, opinions toward a political stimulus may vary widely from strongly favorable to strongly unfavorable. An attempt to map these latent attitudes into, e.g., an "agree-disagree" response format will entail some error. For each category of latent attitude, there is a probability of an agree response and of a disagree response. The concept of an unobservable latent attitude which is probabilistically related to manifest response is derived from Lazarsfeld's (1950) work on stochastic models of attitude structure.

The Wiggins models contain two principal types of parameters: (1) the proportion of respondents in each of a given number of inferred latent attitude classes and (2) the probabilities linking membership in each latent class to the various manifest responses. The latent classes are assumed to be homogeneous in the sense that each person in the class has the same probability of giving a certain manifest response (Wiggins, 1973). Either or both of these sets of parameters may or may not change through discrete time; and the change may be systematic (e.g., Markovian) or not, yielding nine general types of models. Wiggins observed that the models with perhaps the widest application are, first, the one in which neither latent probabilities nor proportions change over time and, second, the model in which latent probabilities remain stable but the proportions in the latent classes change unsystematically from wave to wave.

Most of Wiggins's discussion is in terms of the analysis of dichotomous data, although he shows how the procedure may be extended to polytomies. Assuming a dichotomous response variable with categories labeled 1 and 2, Wiggins adopts the following notation. Let $C_1, C_2, \ldots, C_m$ be the m inferred latent classes at a single point in time and $v_1, v_2, \ldots, v_m$ be the proportions of the sample in each of the m latent classes at that time, where

$$\sum_{i=1}^{m} v_i = 1.$$

These latent proportions form one set of parameters to be estimated. The second set of parameters are the latent probabilities, $a_1, a_2, \ldots, a_m$. Each of these values is the probability that an individual in latent class m will give manifest response 1 (see Figure 2). Last, there are the observed proportions, which for two waves of data are denoted as shown in Table 11.

Given this fundamental model, the observed proportion of the sample giving a 1 response at a single point in time may be decomposed as follows:

$$p_1 = a_1 v_1 + a_2 v_2 + \ldots + a_m v_m. \qquad [1]$$

If latent class proportions are permitted to change over time, then the notation is altered, so that C_{ij} is the class containing individuals in latent class i at t = 1 and in latent class j at t = 2. The corresponding latent proportions are, similarly, v_{ij}. Since a_i is the probability of a 1 response for persons in latent class i and a_j is the probability of a 1 response for persons in latent class j, then $a_i a_j$ is the probability of persons in latent class C_{ij} giving a manifest response of 1 at both t = 1 and t = 2. This statement is based on the assumption of "local independence" of responses, i.e., all respondents in C_j at time t have the same latent probabilities regardless of their class memberships at t − 1. This is a fairly strong assumption, but it is necessary for obtaining unique estimates of the relevant parameters. The observed proportion of individuals giving manifest response 1 at both t = 1 and t = 2 is, therefore,

$$p_{11} = v_{11} a_1 a_1 + v_{12} a_1 a_2 + \ldots + v_{1m} a_1 a_m + \ldots + v_{mm} a_m a_m. \qquad [2]$$

The estimation procedure for the simple model with two waves of observations and no change in either latent proportions or probabilities may now be derived. Note first that since it is assumed that no true change occurs over time, the marginals in Table 11 should be constant, neglecting sampling error: $p_1. = p._1$ and, therefore, $p_2. = p._2$. This implication of the "no true change" model provides a guide to instances in which it is likely to be appropriate. Given the above assumption, the observed turnover table contains only two independent pieces of information; that is, the observed proportions are determined once a cell proportion and a marginal proportion are known.

We shall assume that there are two latent classes. Since it is also assumed that there is no true change, these two latent classes may be denoted C_1 and C_2, with corresponding latent proportion v_1 and v_2. If we arbitrarily select p_{11} and p_1 as the two pieces of information from the observed turnover table, then the following two equations obtain, paralleling Equation 2:

$$p_{11} = v_1 a_1 a_1 + v_2 a_2 a_2 \qquad [3]$$

$$p_{1.} = p_{11} + p_{12} = v_1 a_1 a_1 + v_2 a_2 a_2 + v_1 a_1 (1 - a_1)$$
$$+ v_2 a_2 (1 - a_2). \qquad [4]$$

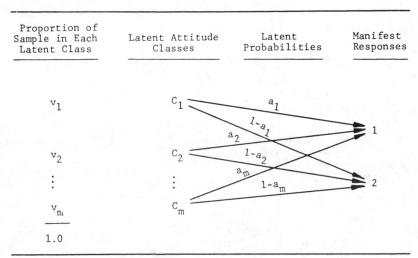

| Proportion of Sample in Each Latent Class | Latent Attitude Classes | Latent Probabilities | Manifest Responses |

Figure 2: Paradigm of Wiggins Model

TABLE 11
Notation of Observed Turnover Proportions for Wiggins Models

		Manifest Response, $t = 2$		
		1	2	
Manifest Response, $t = 1$	1	p_{11}	p_{12}	$p_{1 \cdot}$
	2	p_{21}	p_{22}	$p_{2 \cdot}$
		$p_{\cdot 1}$	$p_{\cdot 2}$	1

We now have three unknowns—a_1, a_2, and v_2 (since $1 - v_2 = v_1$)—but only two independent equations. Therefore, to obtain a unique solution, an additional restriction must be imposed. Wiggins introduces the assumption that the latent probability linking latent category membership to corresponding manifest response is constant across latent classes, i.e.,

$$a_2 = 1 - a_1. \qquad [5]$$

In more conventional terminology, the assumption is that the survey item is equally reliable for individuals regardless of latent attitude. This is a strong assumption, but it is not unusual in most psychometric testing applications, and it may be relaxed in some Wiggins models if more than two waves of data are available.

With Equation 5, Equations 3 and 4 may be simplified into:

$$p_{11} = a_1^2 v_1 + (1 - a_1)^2 v_2$$

$$= a_1^2 (v_1 + v_2) + (1 - 2a_1)v_2$$

$$= a_1^2 + (1 - 2a_1)v_2, \qquad [6]$$

$$p_{1.} = a_1^2 v_1 + (1 - a_1)^2 v_2 + a_1(1 - a_1)v_1$$

$$+ (1 - a_1)a_1 v_2$$

$$= a_1 + (1 - 2a_1)v_2. \qquad [7]$$

By Equation 7,

$$(1 - 2a_1)v_2 = p_{1.} - a_1 \qquad [8]$$

and substituting Equation 8 into 6 yields

$$p_{11} = a_1^2 + p_{1.} - a_1$$

$$a_1^2 - a_1 + (p_{1.} - p_{11}) = 0. \qquad [9]$$

Solving the quadratic Equation 9 for a_1 yields two solutions:

$$a_1 = 1/2 \pm \sqrt{1/4 - (p_{1.} - p_{11})}. \qquad [10]$$

If by convention we posit that persons in C_1 have the larger probability of a 1 response, then the positive root of Equation 10 is taken. Once the estimate of a_1 is secured, the estimate of v_2 (and, thereby, v_1) is obtained from Equation 7.

WIGGINS EXAMPLES

The American panel data in Table 7 appear to meet the "equal marginals" assumption of the "no true change" model. Using Equation 10, the estimated value of a_1 for these data is:

$$a_1 = 1/2 + \sqrt{1/4 - (420/1147 - 286/1147)} = .87,$$

and therefore, $a_2 = 1 - .87 = .13$ by Equation 5. Substitution of a_1 and the observed p_1. into Equation 7 yields:

$$420/1147 = .87 + [1 - 2(.87)]\, v_2,$$

$$v_2 = .68, \text{ and}$$

$$v_1 = 1 - .68 = .32.$$

Thus, assuming that the model is appropriate, the estimated proportions of "true" middle-class and working class identifiers are, respectively, 32% and 68%. The probability that a respondent's latent class and manifest response coincide is estimated to be about .87. For this example, the latter value might be interpreted as the reliability of the survey item.

An example of a Wiggins model in which true change is assumed to occur may be applied to the 1958-1960 American panel data displayed in Table 12. The fit of the black-white model to these data (Table 10) suggested that significantly more movement occurred into the working class category in 1960 than could be accounted for by a no true change model. I shall therefore posit a model in which true change is permissible in the direction of working class identification, but not in the reverse direction. As in the example immediately above, it is assumed that at a single point in time there are two latent classes and that the latent probabilities are complementary and constant over time. The model is summarized in Table 13.

Under the model, the observed transition matrix contains three independent pieces of information, p_{11}, $p_{1\cdot}$, and $p_{\cdot 1}$. From Table 12, the numerical values of these three proportions are .24, .36, and .31, respectively. The equations for these proportions are:

$$p_{1\cdot} = a_1 v_{11} + a_1 v_{12} + (1 - a_1) v_{22} \qquad [11]$$

$$p_{\cdot 1} = a_1 v_{11} + (1 - a_1) v_{12} + (1 - a_1) v_{22} \qquad [12]$$

$$p_{11} = a_1^2 v_{11} + a_1 (1 - a_1) v_{12} + (1 - a_1)^2 v_{22}. \qquad [13]$$

As before, the three equations may be solved for the three unknowns (Wiggins, 1973). The parameter estimates are: $a_1 = .91$, $a_2 = .09$, $v_{11} = .27$, $v_{12} = .06$, and $v_{22} = .67$.

Under this model, the latent probabilities, a_1 and a_2, are roughly comparable to the estimates in the previous example, as is the estimate of the

TABLE 12
Social Class Identification in the United States, 1958-1960

		1960		
		Middle	Working	Total
1958	Middle	.24 (272)	.13 (145)	.36 (417)
	Working	.08 (89)	.56 (641)	.64 (730)
		.31 (361)	.69 (786)	1.00 (1147)

TABLE 13
Summary of Wiggins Model with True Change in One Direction Only

Latent Class	Latent Proportion	Probability of a 1 Response	
		$t = 1$	$t = 2$
c_{11}	v_{11}	a_1	a_1
c_{12}	v_{12}	a_1	$1 - a_1$
c_{21}	0	$1 - a_1$	a_1
c_{22}	v_{22}	$1 - a_1$	$1 - a_1$

proportion of stable working class identifiers, v_{11}. However, a sizable fraction of the 1958 latent middle class is estimated to have shifted to latent working class identification by 1960: $v_{12} = .06$.

EVALUATION OF THE WIGGINS MODEL

These two examples demonstrate the ideas underlying the Wiggins family of models. The models have the advantage of being relatively flexible, enabling the researcher to incorporate his or her a priori assumptions about change at both manifest and latent levels. As Beck (1975) pointed out, Wiggins models make explicit the confluence of true change and response error in panel data. At the same time, however, they possess certain drawbacks which have probably inhibited broader use. First, as is the case with simple Markov chains, Wiggins models possess no explanatory power. They *represent* change processes mathematically, they do not explain them. In addition, estimation procedures often require fairly precise a priori assumptions about latent classes and probabilities which are not readily testable. A related point is that, as Wiggins himself recognized, the models provide no measure of goodness of fit by which they may be evaluated. This is a serious problem, although for models with more independent equations than unknowns, a chi-square procedure similar to that described for Markov models could probably be applied. Finally, from a more technical perspective, the estimation procedures have yet to be computerized, and handling variables other than dichotomies becomes unwieldly. Despite these disadvantages, the Wiggins models may provide valuable insights into the nature of the dynamic process under study, and they ought to be included in a panel researcher's repertoire of analytical strategies.

Coleman Model

Coleman's (1964a, 1964b) approach to the analysis of panel data is similar to Wiggins's in that it recognizes that manifest change may include error—response uncertainty, in Coleman's language—as well as true change. The two families of models differ in some significant ways, however, both in terms of the theories of attitude change from which they are derived and, consequently, in the parameters to be estimated.

Coleman's model is based on the idea that an individual's latent attitude is composed of a (possibly large) number of attitude *elements*, each of which is conditioned to a particular response state at any point in time. For example, an individual's latent attitude toward a political candidate may be thought of as being decomposable into attitude elements associated with the candidate's personal characteristics, issue positions, experience, and so on. Each of these attitude elements is assumed to move through a set of response states i, $i = 1, 2, \ldots, s$, according to a first-order Markov scheme. The response states are simply the various possible responses to a particular survey item. Thus, for Coleman, attitude change occurs fundamentally at the level of attitude elements, not at the level of individuals themselves.

For a dichotomous response stimulus, if m_0 attitude elements favor response 0 and m_1 elements favor response 1 at time t, then the probability of the individual giving response 0 equals the proportion of elements in response state 0:

$$\Pr\{R_0\} = v_{0t} = m_0/(m_0 + m_1). \qquad [14]$$

The space through which attitude elements move is discrete, i.e., it is comprised of the possible response states. But since the number of attitude elements may be large, the attitude space of individuals, i.e., the possible gradations of latent attitude, is essentially continuous. In the example of a dichotomous response variable, the individual's latent attitude may be at any point along a 0 – 1 continuum, depending on his or her particular mix of elements m_0 and m_1. This representation of latent attitudes as continuous is an advantage of the Coleman model over the Wiggins model, although it should be noted that the Wiggins models permit more latent attitude classes than there are manifest response states.

Another difference between the Coleman model and other approaches discussed thus far is that the former assumes that the Markov process governing change in elements is continuous rather than discrete in time. A continuous time Markov process is governed by a matrix Q of transition intensities q_{ij}, which can be thought of as instantaneous rates of transfer between states. If a fixed time interval t is allowed to pass, the q_{ij} determine a matrix of transition probabilities R(t). Each $r_{ij(t)}$ is the probability that an element in state i at time 0 is in state j at time t (Coleman, 1964a, 1964b).[3] As was shown in the discussion of discrete time Markov processes, the proportion of elements in response state j at time t, v_{jt}, is:

$$v_{jt} = v_{10} r_{1j(t)} + v_{20} r_{2j(t)} + \ldots + v_{j0} r_{jj(t)}$$
$$+ \ldots + v_{s0} r_{sj(t)}. \qquad [15]$$

The empirical problem that remains is to use data on individual response turnover to infer transition probabilities at the level of elements (Coleman, 1964b). If one knew the marginal distribution of individuals in terms of their v_{jt}, symbolized $f(v_{jt})$, then the proportion of individuals giving response j at time t would be:[4]

$$p_{jt} = \int_0^1 v_{jt} f(v_{jt}) \, dv_j. \qquad [16]$$

Equation 16 links the observed proportions, p_{jt}, to the unobservable proportions, v_{jt}, which are in turn related to R(t) by Equation 15. Extending this line of argument, Coleman (1964b) shows that if we have three-wave panel data (waves labeled 0, 1, and 2) where the time interval between waves 1 and 2 is t, then:

$$p_{i \cdot j} = p_{i1} \cdot r_{1j(t)} + p_{i2} \cdot r_{2j(t)} + \ldots + p_{is} \cdot r_{sj(t)}, \qquad [17]$$

where $p_{i \cdot j}$ is the observed proportion of individuals giving response i in wave 0 and response j in wave 2, p_{i1}. is the proportion responding i in wave 0 and 1 in wave 1, and so on.

There will be an equation similar to Equation 17 for each combination of response i in wave 0 and response j in wave 2. In matrix notation,

$$P(0,2) = P(0,1)R(t), \qquad [18]$$

where all matrices are s × s. This system of equations may then be solved for the $r_{ij(t)}$:

$$R(t) = P(0,1)^{-1}P(0,2). \qquad [19]$$

Once the time-specific $R(t)$ matrix has been estimated, the Q matrix of transition intensities may be derived. Conceptually, the process involves shrinking the time span upon which $R(t)$ is based to a limiting value of zero (Beck, 1975). Coleman (1964b) described the details of the operational procedure. Coleman has written a computer program to estimate $R(t)$, Q, and certain other values which are by-products of the Coleman scheme.

To reiterate, both $R(t)$ and Q refer to true change at the level of the element; therefore, the concepts of response error and reliability do not apply. Once we move to the level of individuals, however, we face the possibility that the relationship between latent attitude and manifest response is confounded by error. A reasonable definition of unreliability is the change between measurements taken sufficiently close in time so as to preclude any true change. Building on this definition, Coleman derives reliability coefficients by taking the observed individual turnover matrix and calculating the transition probabilities as the time interval between waves shrinks to zero. Assuming that the time intervals between waves are equal, this is accomplished as follows. If we conceive of the matrix $P(0,0)$ as the turnover matrix with the time lag reaching zero as a limit, then it follows directly from Equation 18 that:

$$P(0,1) = P(0,0)R(t). \qquad [20]$$

Once $R(t)$ has been estimated, it, together with the observed $P(0,1)$ matrix, yields an estimate of $P(0,0)$:

$$P(0,0) = P(0,1)R(t)^{-1}. \qquad [21]$$

The elements on the main diagonal of P(0,0) may be thought of as reliability coefficients for wave 0. An analogous procedure is used to estimate P(1,1) and P(2,2).

The final information to be derived is an estimate of the distribution V of latent attitudes. As mentioned earlier, for a dichotomous response variable this would be a continuous distribution along the interval 0-1. For a variety of theoretical and mathematical reasons, Coleman (1964b) chose to use the family of contagious binomial distributions to represent V. This distribution has the advantage that when response uncertainty is low, most individuals will be located near the extremes of the distribution; and when response uncertainty is high, individuals will be located all along the continuum. The contagious binomial distribution is determined by two parameters which are functions of the transition intensities. The distribution is defined under the assumption that the process is in equilibrium. The reader is referred to Coleman (1964a, 1964b) for a discussion of the contagious binomial and its use in the present context.

COLEMAN MODEL EXAMPLE

The Coleman model is specifically designed for the analysis of processes which may be characterized as Markovian, possibly confounded by error. Moreover, its application requires at least three waves of data. Because of these restrictions, the Coleman approach should only be utilized in situations for which a simple Markov scheme (obscured by error) appears to hold through a period containing at least three sets of observations. This situation is characterized by roughly stable marginals in the turn-over tables and stable or declining values along the main diagonals as the time span between waves increases. The data on British social class identification in Table 14 appear to meet the requirements of the Coleman model, and so they will form the basis of this example.

Table 15 shows the estimated matrix of transition probabilities as calculated using Equation 19. Based on these results, attitude elements (and hence individual class identification) tended to be quite stable during the time period under study. Most of the observed change is due to response uncertainty. The reliabilities are quite constant across waves, equal to about .70 and .89 for middle and working classes, respectively. Last, the estimated equilibrium distribution of latent class identification is displayed in Figure 3. The distribution exhibits a concentration at the working class end of the continuum and a smaller clustering at the opposite extreme. This is as we would expect given the small probabilities of change contained in R(t); see Table 15.

TABLE 14
Observed Proportions, British Social Class Identification,
1963-1964 and 1963-1966

| | | Wave 1 | | |
		Middle	Working	Total
Wave 0	Middle	.199	.064	.263
	Working	.094	.643	.737
		.293	.707	1.000

| | | Wave 2 | | |
		Middle	Working	Total
Wave 0	Middle	.194	.069	.263
	Working	.094	.643	.737
		.288	.712	1.000

TABLE 15
Coleman Model Estimates for the British Social Class Data

| R (t): | | | Time t | |
			Middle Working	
	Time 0	Middle	.998	.002
		Working	.026	.974

| Reliabilities | | Wave | | |
		0	1	2
Middle class		.71	.70	.70
Working class		.88	.89	.89

EVALUATION OF THE COLEMAN MODEL

The Coleman approach possesses a number of distinct advantages over both simple Markov chain models and the Wiggins variant. An explicit model of attitude change underlies the Coleman model, and the

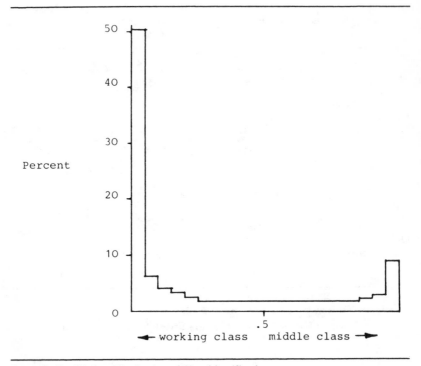

Figure 3: Equilibrium Distribution of Class Identification

conceptualization of latent attitudes as continuous is an improvement over Wiggins's use of discrete latent attitude classes. Moreover, Coleman (1964b) has extended this method to permit the introduction of independent variables which influence the transition rates.

A price is paid for these advances, however. Coleman's strategy requires three waves of data, and, more important, Coleman (1964b) explicitly designed his model to fit change data displaying the "empirical regularity" of a Markov process obscured by response uncertainty. The assumption that change in attitude elements is first-order Markovian in nature is quite restrictive, and the Coleman model should only be used in situations for which this simple change model is theoretically plausible. In practice, there are many empirical patterns of change that do not fit the assumptions of the Coleman model, and in such cases the inappropriateness of the model is evidenced in implausible parameter estimates or, in extreme instances, by a failure to produce any estimates at all. To provide just one example, the American panel data on social class identification used in earlier examples are not consistent with the empirical patterns implied by the Coleman model. Last, it should be noted that, as with the Wiggins models, the Coleman approach provides no method of assessing goodness of fit, although chi-square tests are, in principle, applicable.

In sum, the Coleman model is a powerful analytical strategy, logically derived from an explicit model of attitude change. As such, it will be of great use in situations that meet its restrictive set of assumptions. If the change process under study does not display the "empirical regularity" presumed by Coleman's method, however, the researcher should employ an alternative analytical strategy.

Log-Linear Models

A final alternative approach to the analysis of categorical panel data consists of the system for the analysis of multivariate contingency tables devised by Goodman (1970, 1972a, 1972b). The Goodman method can be applied to polytomous data, although it is probably best suited to variables that are dichotomous. Also, the method does not require panel data and may even be applied in situations in which relationships exist among a set of variables but no distinction is made between independent and dependent variables (Goodman, 1970, 1972a). A special case of the general model occurs when the researcher is able to posit some causal ordering of variables (Goodman, 1972b, 1973, 1976). Since the temporal structure of panel data usually permits some a priori specification of dependent versus independent variables, and since a treatment of the general model can become complex, I shall restrict my attention to the special case.

Broadly speaking, the Goodman technique estimates and tests the significance of the effects of one or more independent variables on the odds favoring assignment to a particular category of the dependent variable. Because it enables the delineation and testing of different models of change, the Goodman approach possesses some definite advantages over other analytical models described thus far. No method is without its drawbacks, however, and, as will be discussed, this is true with respect to log-linear analysis as well.

As with the more traditional chi-square tests to which it is related, the data to be analyzed by Goodman's log-linear procedure consist of the cell frequencies in a multivariate cross-classification design. The computational details of the procedure are not enlightening, and they are discussed elsewhere (Goodman, 1970, 1972a; Bishop et al., 1975). A brief exposition of the logic of the analytical approach is useful, however.

Consider the example in Table 16, where variables A, B, and C are, respectively, a binary control variable (such as respondent's sex) and the time 1 and time 2 responses to some dichotomous response variable of interest (for example, favoring or opposing a proposed law). Variable C is, therefore, the dependent variable.[5] Let the numbers 1 and 2 denote the two categories of each variable; and a, b, ..., h are the observed internal cell frequencies.

For individuals for whom A = 1 and B = 1, the observed odds favoring response C = 1 may be calculated as a/b. Similarly, the observed odds of being in category 1 of the dependent variable given that A = i and B = j (symbolized ω_{ij}) is:

$$\omega_{11} = a/b \qquad\qquad \omega_{21} = e/f$$

$$\omega_{12} = c/d \qquad\qquad \omega_{22} = g/h. \qquad [22]$$

In a manner paralleling the classical analysis of variance (ANOVA) model (Hays, 1973; Iversen and Norpoth, 1976) the expected odds (as opposed to the observed odds in Equation 22) under a given model, Ω_{ij}, may be described as the product of "main effects" and "interaction effects" pertaining to the explanatory variables. In Goodman's notation, the full or "saturated" model containing all possible effects for the present example would be:

$$\Omega_{ij} = \gamma \cdot \gamma_i^A \cdot \gamma_j^B \cdot \gamma_{ij}^{AB}, \qquad [23]$$

where γ, γ_i^A, γ_j^B denote the main effects on Ω_{ij} of the grand mean and variables A and B, respectively, and where γ_{ij}^{AB} represents the interaction effect. A difference between Equation 23 and the usual ANOVA model is that the former is multiplicative in the effects coefficients whereas the latter is an additive model. As will be seen shortly, however, Equation 23 can be easily transformed into an additive model. Interpretation of the effects coefficients is best put off until that transformation is made.

Since the predictor variables are binary, the following limitations are imposed on the effects:

$$\gamma_2^A = 1/\gamma_1^A, \quad \gamma_2^B = 1/\gamma_1^B \qquad [24]$$

$$\gamma_{11}^{AB} = \gamma_{22}^{AB} = 1/\gamma_{12}^{AB} = 1/\gamma_{21}^{AB}. \qquad [25]$$

These restrictions parallel the restrictions in the ANOVA model that the effects associated with categories of an independent variable sum to zero,

TABLE 16
Hypothetical Cross-Classification of Variables A, B, and C

	A = 1			A = 2	
	B = 1	B = 2		B = 1	B = 2
C = 1	a	c	C = 1	e	g
C = 2	b	d	C = 2	f	h

as does the sum of interaction effects. Since Equation 23 is multiplicative rather than additive, the product, rather than the sum, of effects is constrained to "cancel out," i.e., to equal unity (Hays, 1973; Iversen and Norpoth, 1976).

The full model is referred to as "saturated" because it includes as many effects as there are degrees of freedom in the cross-classification and, hence, reproduces the observed odds exactly. If, on theoretical or empirical grounds, certain effects were determined to be trivial, then the appropriate γ terms would be removed from the model. The expected odds generated by the revised model would then differ from the observed values, and the significance of this difference could be evaluated via the usual chi-square test for comparing an expected contingency table under a specific model with the observed cell frequencies (Goodman, 1972a, 1972b; Davis, 1974). Generally, the researcher attempts to develop a model which is parsimonious while still maintaining a close fit to the data.

In theory, it would be possible to devise a model containing interaction effects but no main effects. In practice, however, permissible models are restricted by the hierarchy principle (Reynolds, 1977): If higher order interactions of variables are included in a particular model, then all lower order effects containing these variables must also be included. Thus, in the present example if we wish to retain the γ_{ij}^{AB} interaction effect, then both main effects must also be included.

The multiplicative-effects model (Equation 23) for the odds ratio can be expressed as an equivalent additive effects model by taking natural logarithms of both sides of the equation, yielding:

$$\log \Omega_{ij} = \Phi_{ij} = \beta + \beta_i^A + \beta_j^B + \beta_{ij}^{AB}, \qquad [26]$$

where the β coefficients are the logarithms of the corresponding γ coefficients in Equation 23. The symbol Φ_{ij} is called the "log-odds," hence the common reference to the Goodman approach as a "log-odds" or "log-linear" model. In addition,

$$\beta_2^A = -\beta_1^A, \quad \beta_2^B = -\beta_1^B \tag{27}$$

$$\beta_{11}^{AB} = \beta_{22}^{AB} = -\beta_{12}^{AB} = -\beta_{21}^{AB}. \tag{28}$$

Equations 26 to 28 become more meaningful if they are compared with the usual ANOVA model. The primary conceptual difference is that the ANOVA model represents the effects of treatment variables on an interval level criterion measure whereas Equation 26 uses the logarithm of the odds favoring classification in a particular category of the dependent variable as the criterion. Once this conceptual shift is made, the interpretation of the β coefficients becomes reasonably straightforward. The coefficient β is simply the mean of the ϕ_{ij}—in the example, the mean of the logarithms of the four ω_{ij} values in Equation 22. The β_i^A and β_j^B coefficients represent deviations from this mean log-odds value resulting from being in the ith category of variable A or the jth category of variable B, respectively. The β_{ij}^{AB} term is the interaction effect due to concurrent location in category A = i and B = j. Equations 27 and 28 indicate that, as in the ANOVA model, the sum of deviations from the mean due to each main effect equals zero, as does the sum of interaction effects.

Estimates of the Φ_{ij} for a given model, and thereby the β values, are obtained via an iterative maximum likelihood approach described in the sources cited above. An intuitive understanding of the method may be gained by comparing the log-linear system with a multiple regression approach to the analytical problem.

LOG-LINEAR REGRESSION MODELS

Consider the following regression-type model, in which Z_1 equals 1 when A = 1 and Z_1 equals −1 when A = 2; in which Z_2 is 1 when B = 1 and −1 when B = 2; and in which $Z_3 = Z_1 Z_2$:

$$\Phi_{ij} = \beta_0 + \beta_1 Z_1 + \beta_2 Z_2 + \beta_3 Z_3. \tag{29}$$

Since Equation 29 is the saturated model for the present example (and hence will reproduce the observed log-odds exactly), there is no disturbance term attached to the regression equation. A comparison of Equation 29 with Equations 26 to 28 shows that they are equivalent ways of describing the same model, with

$$\beta_0 = \beta, \quad \beta_1 = \beta_1^A, \quad \beta_2 = \beta_1^B, \quad \text{and} \quad \beta_3 = \beta_{11}^{AB}. \tag{30}$$

Similarly, the nonsaturated model,

$$\Phi_{ij} = \beta + \beta_i^A + \beta_j^B, \qquad [31]$$

is equivalent to the regression equation,

$$\Phi_{ij} = \beta_0 + \beta_1 Z_1 + \beta_2 Z_2 + e_{ij}, \qquad [32]$$

where e_{ij} is the disturbance term. The expected values of the ordinary least squares (OLS) estimates of the β's in Equation 32 are identical to those of the iterative maximum likelihood estimates of the corresponding coefficients in Equation 31.

As Goodman points out, however, the disturbance in Equation 32 is not homoscedastic and, therefore, OLS will yield inefficient parameter estimates; in addition, the usual significance tests of the β coefficients do not apply (see Kmenta, 1971).[7] Grizzle et al. (1969) suggest a weighted least-squares procedure to counteract these problems (see also, Hanushek and Jackson, 1977). In practice, however, evidence suggests that heteroscedasticity will have little effect on the efficiency of the OLS estimator unless many of the conditional percentage splits on the dependent variable in a multivariate contingency table are extreme. A split of 25%/75% is quite conservative as a boundary for "extreme," and even 10%/90% is probably acceptable for most purposes (see Goodman, 1976; Gillespie, 1977).

LOG-LINEAR ANALYSIS EXAMPLE

In the section on Markov processes, I presented data indicating that changes in perceived financial status influenced the stability of social class identification in the United States (Table 6). We shall now analyze these same data by the log-odds method, with one additional variable included. That variable is whether or not the respondents view social class as being salient to themselves. This variable is introduced to determine if the effect of perceived financial status on class identification is relatively stronger among respondents for whom the notion of social classes is particularly salient. That is, we are interested in the presence of an interaction between saliency of social class and financial status.

The relevant data are presented in Table 17. It is readily apparent from the table that class identification is correlated with itself from one time point to the next. There is also some indication of the hypothesized interaction effect: For the high salience group, the probability of a stable response is .85 for middle-class respondents whose financial status has improved and only .49 for middle-class respondents whose finances were

TABLE 17

Cross-Classification of Class Saliency, Perceived Financial Change, and Class Identification, United States, 1956-1958

	High Salience (A=1)				Low Salience (A=2)			
	Better Off (B=1)		Worse Off (B=2)		Better Off (B=1)		Worse Off (B=2)	
	1956		1956		1956		1956	
	M (C=1)	W (C=2)	M (C=1)	W (C=2)	M (C=1)	W (C=2)	M (C=1)	W (C=2)
1958								
Middle	.85 (56)	.21 (16)	.49 (17)	.08 (5)	.74 (37)	.23 (10)	.73 (11)	.18 (2)
Working	.15 (10)	.79 (61)	.51 (18)	.92 (57)	.26 (13)	.77 (34)	.27 (4)	.82 (9)

perceived to have changed for the worse; within the low-salience group, in contrast, the corresponding probabilities are virtually identical regardless of the direction of perceived financial change, .74 versus .73.

The log-linear analysis enables us to evaluate these effects more precisely. We will proceed by first calculating the coefficients for the saturated log-odds model, i.e., the model which reproduces the frequencies in Table 17 exactly. We shall then eliminate those effects terms which are trival and estimate the revised model. A chi-square test will show whether the simplified model maintains a close fit to the observed frequencies.

The coefficients for the saturated model may be calculated directly from the observed data in Table 17 (Goodman, 1972b).[8] The estimating equations are of the form:

$$\hat{\beta} = \sum_i \sum_j \sum_k \Phi_{ijk}/8 \qquad [33]$$

$$\hat{\beta}_1^A = [\sum_j \sum_k (\Phi_{1jk} - \Phi_{2jk})/4]/2 \qquad [34]$$

$$\hat{\beta}_1^B = \sum_i \sum_k (\Phi_{i1k} - \Phi_{i2k})/8 \qquad [35]$$

$$\hat{\beta}_{11}^{AB} = \sum_k (\Phi_{11k} + \Phi_{22k} - \Phi_{12k} - \Phi_{21k})/8 \qquad [36]$$

$$\hat{\beta}_{111}^{ABC} = (\Phi_{111} + \Phi_{221} + \Phi_{212} + \Phi_{122} - \Phi_{222}$$

$$- \Phi_{112} - \Phi_{121} - \Phi_{211})/8. \qquad [37]$$

As can be seen from Equation 33, $\hat{\beta}$ is the mean of the Φ_{ijk}. Equation 34 shows that $\hat{\beta}_1^A$ is one-half of the mean difference between Φ_{1jk} and Φ_{2jk}. A similar interpretation can be given to Equation 35 and to the equation for $\hat{\beta}_1^C$, not shown, which has a corresponding form. Basically similar interpretations can be made of the equations for the various interaction terms. The equations for $\hat{\beta}_{11}^{AC}$ and $\hat{\beta}_{11}^{BC}$ have forms that parallel Equation 36.

In addition, an estimated standard error for the $\hat{\beta}$ coefficients can be calculated:

$$SE_{\hat{\beta}} = [(\sum_i \sum_j \sum_k \sum_l 1/f_{ijkl})/64]^{1/2}, \qquad [38]$$

where the subscript l refers to the levels of the dependent variable and f means "cell frequency." Thus, the numerator of Equation 38 is simply the sum of the inverses of the 16 cell frequencies in Table 17. The ratio of each effects coefficient to the estimated standard error forms a t ratio which can be used to test the null hypothesis that an effect is not significantly different from zero (Goodman, 1972b).

The coefficients for the saturated model are displayed in Table 18A. These results indicate that the A × C, B × C, and A × B × C interaction terms are nonsignificant and may be deleted from the model. The A main effect is also fairly small, but since we wish to retain the A × B interaction, the hierarchical modeling principle requires that this main effect be retained along with the significant B and C main effects. The coefficients for the revised model are shown in Table 18B. All effects are significant at the .05 level (one-tailed), and the small chi-square value indicates that the cell frequencies generated by the model diverge very little from the observed frequencies; that is, the revised model fits the observed data well.

Interpretation of the numerical values of the estimates in Table 18 is somewhat problematic, since they refer to changes in the log-odds of middle-class identification. However, one way of gaining some insight into the strength of the estimated effects, in particular the interaction effect, is to calculate the net change in the log-odds of middle-class identification predicted by the model for different levels of variables A and B. These predictions, obtained by using the equalities described by Equations 27 and 28, are displayed in Table 19. The table shows that, within the high-salience category, there is an expected difference of 1.24 in the log-odds favoring middle-class identification for the better financial change group versus the worse financial change group. In contrast, within the low-salience category, the expected net effects are identical for B = 1 and B = 2. These implications are entirely consistent with the observed frequencies in Table 18.

AN ALTERNATIVE MODEL

Recall that both Equations 26 and 29 employ the frequencies from a set of cross-classifications as the input data rather than the individual cases themselves. An alternative model would be:

$$Y = \beta_0' + \beta_1' Z_1 + \beta_2' Z_2 + \beta_3' Z_3 + e, \qquad [39]$$

where Z_1, Z_2, and Z_3 are defined as before but with respect to individual respondents rather than cells and where Y is a dummy variable coded 1 for respondents when C = 1 and coded 0 when C = 2.

A major difference between Equation 39 and the earlier models is that Equation 39 is a linear model for the probability of being in class 1 of the dependent variable (or, in the aggregate, for the proportion of re-

TABLE 18
Log-Odds Analysis of 1958 Social Class Identification

A. Saturated Model.

Effect	$\hat{\beta}$	t-ratio
Constant	−.35	−2.12
A	−.18	−1.10
B	.40	2.44
C	1.28	7.81
AB	.32	1.96
AC	.08	.50
BC	.05	.34
ABC	.12	.71

B. Revised Model.

Effect	$\hat{\beta}$	t-ratio
Constant	−.31	−1.92
A	−.30	−1.88
B	.31	1.92
C	1.29	7.97
AB	.31	1.92

$\chi^2 = 4.76$, df = 6, $\alpha > .50$

A = Class saliency.
B = Financial situation.
C = 1956 class identification.

TABLE 19
Expected Change in Log-Odds Favoring Middle-Class
Identification, by Levels of A and B

Effect	High Salience (A=1)		Low Salience (A=2)	
	Better Off (B=1)	Worse Off (B=2)	Better Off (B=1)	Worse Off (B=2)
A	−.30	−.30	.30	.30
B	.31	−.31	.31	−.31
AB	.31	−.31	−.31	.31
Net	.32	−.92	.30	.30

spondents in class 1 of variable C), while the earlier models are linear in the log-odds favoring C = 1. As Figure 4 demonstrates, probability and log-odds are nonlinearly related, but the relationship is very nearly linear in the range $.25 < p < .75$ and is approximately linear in the range $.10 < p < .90$. Hence the dummy dependent-variable model and the log-odds models will yield similar conclusions so long as the conditional splits on the dependent variable are not extreme.

Ordinary least-squares estimation of Equation 39 faces two problems: (1) the heteroscedasticity of the disturbance and (2) the bounded nature of the dependent variable (as opposed to the unbounded range of log-odds). As already mentioned, the first problem is of practical consequence primarily in situations wherein dependent variable splits are extreme, and in such instances Equation 39 is probably not appropriate anyway (Gillespie, 1977; Hanushek and Jackson, 1977). The second problem is that predicted values of the dependent variable may fall outside the permissible 0-1 bounds. From an applied perspective this drawback may be mitigated simply by truncating $\hat{Y}$ values that exceed the bounds $0 \leqslant \hat{Y} \leqslant 1$ (Kmenta, 1971).

EXAMPLE OF THE DUMMY DEPENDENT-VARIABLE MODEL

Table 20 displays the results of an OLS estimation of a model like Equation 39 as applied to the American social class panel data. When these results are compared with the log-odds analysis in Table 18, it is apparent that both approaches indicate that the B, C, and AB effects are significant in the saturated model (Table 20A). Similarly, the revised regression results (Tables 20B and 21) show that essentially the same substantive conclusions would be reached from either the log-odds or the dummy variable analysis.

EVALUATION OF THE GOODMAN AND DUMMY DEPENDENT-VARIABLE MODELS

Despite the potential estimation problems associated with Equation 39, the dummy dependent-variable model has some advantages that are worth considering. First, it permits the incorporation of continuus as well as polytomous independent variables; continuous variables must be collapsed before they can be handled by the Goodman procedure, resulting in a loss of information. Second, the coefficients in Equation 39 have a simple interpretation as probability increments, in contrast to the less straightforward interpretation of log-odds parameters. In addition,

TABLE 20
Dummy Dependent-Variable Analysis of 1958 Social Class Identification

A. Saturated Model.

Effect	$\hat{\beta}$	t-ratio
Constant	.44	16.75
A	−.03	−1.24
B	.07	2.59
C	.26	10.08
AB	.05	2.09
AC	−.00	−.09
BC	.02	.94
ABC	.03	1.31

B. Revised Model.

Effect	$\hat{\beta}$	t-ratio
Constant	.44	17.08
A	−.03	−1.10
B	.06	2.38
C	.27	12.59
AB	.05	1.91

A = Class saliency.
B = Financial situation.
C = 1956 class identification.

TABLE 21
Expected Change in Probability of Middle-Class
Identification, by Levels of A and B

Effect	High Salience (A=1)		Low Salience (A=2)	
	Better Off (B=1)	Worse Off (B=2)	Better Off (B=1)	Worse Off (B=2)
A	−.03	−.03	.03	.03
B	.06	−.06	.06	−.06
AB	.05	−.05	−.05	.05
Net	.08	−.14	.04	.02

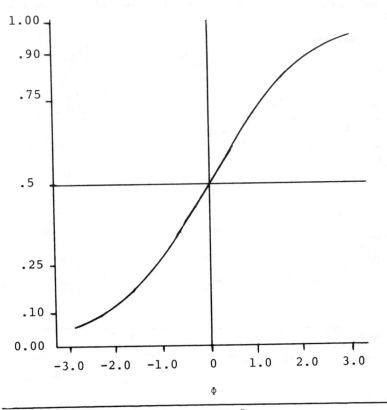

Figure 4: Graph of Probability, P, versus Log-Odds, Φ

Equation 39 can be incorporated into a system of simultaneous equations; and, if required, one may apply estimators appropriate for such systems, e.g., two-stage least squares (Gillespie, 1977). If other requirements are met, models such as Equation 39 may also be estimated by procedures which take into account the presence of errors in the variables (Blalock, 1970; Duncan, 1972). The Goodman log-linear model has not been extended to cover these situations, although it perhaps could be (e.g., Hanushek and Jackson, 1977).

Given these considerations, the final choice of analytical procedure will probably be determined by the complexity of the system of variables under study, by the theoretical appropriateness of a model that is linear in the probabilities or in the log-odds, and by the array of estimation techniques available to the researcher.

3. ANALYSIS OF INTERVAL LEVEL VARIABLES

The previous section was devoted to methods of analysis which are appropriate when measurement entails as little as the classification of cases into a few discrete categories. If, on the other hand, the measurement process yields data which satisfy interval level requirements, analytical procedures based on the multiple regression model naturally come to the fore, and in this section the emphasis will be on the use of such procedures with panel data. I shall discuss first some of the advantages of a multiple regression approach versus other strategies, then we will explore some complications which may arise when regression techniques are applied to longitudinal social data. Last, a relatively new method of data analysis which merges aspects of multiple regression with factor-analytic approaches is described.

Regression Effects

Perhaps the most straightforward way to proceed with a discussion of regression effects is within the context of a concrete example, an investigation of the effect of military service on feelings of trust toward the national government (Jennings and Markus, 1977). One research strategy would be to conduct a survey and compare the scores on an index of political trust for respondents who had served in the armed forces with those of respondents with no such experience. An obvious flaw in this approach is that the two groups may have differed initially on the dependent variable. For example, veterans may have been relatively more trusting of government even before they were recruited, and a sound research design should control for such a possibility.

One of the advantages of a panel study is that it can provide the relevant "pretest" information. In the Jennings and Markus research, a national sample of 1,348 young adults was interviewed in 1965 (when they were high school seniors) and then again in 1973. A five-item measure of political trust was administered in each wave. In the reinterview it was determined that 328 respondents had engaged in some active military service since their graduation.

One method of controlling for initial trust levels would be to calculate the change in political trust for each individual,

$$\Delta Y = Y_2 - Y_1,$$

where Y_t is the score on variable Y at time t, and then compare the average change scores of the service and nonservice groups. Unfortunately, this seemingly uncomplicated procedure is fraught with difficulties. The crux of the problem is that the change scores will *not* be independent of the initial values (as they ought to be had we truly controlled for time 1 scores), but instead will be negatively correlated with them. This fact is well known (Thorndike, 1924; Campbell and Stanley, 1963; Lord, 1963; Bohrnstedt, 1969)—indeed, it gave regression analysis its name—but the implications have apparently been overlooked in a good deal of social research.

In terms of the present example, the implications can be spelled out quite simply. If veterans had somewhat higher time 1 trust scores than did members of the control group, then the former will display relatively smaller gains under the null hypothesis of no service effect. Hence if we ignored the *regression effect*, we might well conclude that military experience had a deleterious influence on political trust when, in truth, the null hypothesis is correct.

The regression effect is no mystical phenomenon. Nor is it uniquely the result of measurement error, as is sometimes mistakenly believed. It is a consequence of the less than perfect correlation between the values of a variable at two points in time. Consider a variable which can be measured with sufficient accuracy so that errors of measurement may be safely ignored, such as weight. The weights of individuals measured at two reasonably separate points in time will not correlate at unity, due to the effects of the stochastic factors (food intake, state of health, and so on) summarized in the disturbance term of the equation:

$$W_2 = \alpha + \beta W_1 + e_2. \qquad [40]$$

If we assume that the disturbance is distributed approximately normally with mean zero, then at time 1, individuals weighing more than the overall mean will include a disproportionate number of persons for whom the disturbance term takes on a positive value, i. e., above its mean of zero. For those persons, at time 2 the odds favor that the value of the stochastic term will be less than it was at time 1 (see Figure 5). In plain language, the expectation is that the heavy individuals at time 1 will weigh less at time 2. Similarly, persons of below average weight at time 1 will tend to exhibit a weight gain when remeasured, thus the expectation of regression toward the mean or, equivalently, negative correlation between initial score and subsequent change.[9]

It should be noted that the regression effect does not imply a shrinkage in variance over time. If the system is in equilibrium, the *expected* (or predicted) time 2 values will have smaller variance than the time 1 values, but the *actual* (expected plus disturbance) values will possess the same variance as the initial scores.

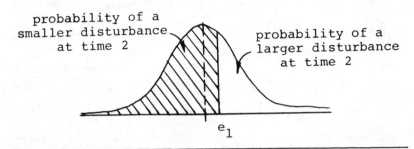

Figure 5: Probability Distribution of e_t

Some researchers apparently believe that change attributable to regression effects is not "true" change. This is not correct. If an individual's weight differs by two kilos on successive weighings, then this is true change, so long as the scale is accurate.[10] The point is not whether the change is true (it is), but rather that we take care not to attribute regression effects to the influence of the independent variable in the study.

We began by searching for an analytical strategy for determining the effects of military service on political trust. We decided that it was important to control for initial trust levels but that the calculation of change scores was an unsatisfactory method for achieving this end. Where does this leave us? The usual statistical procedure for eliminating the effects of a third variable is partial correlation or multiple regression, and this applies to panel data as well.[11] Correlational methods are sensitive to changes in variances across populations, thereby rendering comparisons problematic, while unstandardized regression techniques are not. The latter are, therefore, generally preferred (Blalock, 1967; Bohrnstedt, 1969).

For the example, the relevant regression equation is:

$$Y_2 = \alpha + \beta_1 Y_1 + \beta_2 M + e_2. \qquad [41]$$

Where M is a binary variable coded to distinguish veterans from non-veterans.[12] If the disturbance satisfies the necessary assumptions, the OLS estimate of β_2 will provide the best estimate of the effect of service experience on political trust.[13] And the t ratio of $\hat{\beta}_2$ to its estimated standard error yields the appropriate test of significance.

It is useful to recognize that the change score approach is simply a special case of Equation 41 wherein β_1 is assumed to equal unity:

$$\Delta Y = Y_2 - Y_1 = \alpha + \beta M + e_2$$

$$Y_2 = \alpha + Y_1 + \beta M + e_2. \qquad [42]$$

Since there is nothing to be gained (and much to be lost) by constraining β_1 to equal 1.0, Equation 41 is clearly preferable to Equation 42. As Cronbach and Furby put it: "There appears to be no need to use measures of change as dependent variables and no virtue in using them" (1970: 78).

In the next section, I extend the discussion of multiple regression to cases in which a number of equations are linked to represent a causal scheme.

Causal Inference

The functional interconnections among variables are likely to be complex for most social processes, making it difficult if not impossible to ascertain unambiguously "what causes what" on the basis of data collected at a single point in time. A major advantage (as well as a potential problem) of panel data is the ability "to exploit inter-temporal variation in such a way as to simplify causal inference" (Hannan and Young, 1977: 54).

Early efforts at causal analysis of panel data emphasized cross-lagged correlational designs of various sorts (Campbell and Clayton, 1961; Campbell, 1963; Yee and Gage, 1968; Rozelle and Campbell, 1969; Shingles, 1976). Using the example of the two-variable, two-wave situation in Figure 6, the idea behind cross-lagged panel analysis was to compare the magnitudes of $r_{X_1Y_2}$ and $r_{Y_1X_2}$ to determine the dominant direction of causal effect between X and Y. The four path coefficients in Figure 6 are the standardized regression coefficients linking time 2 values of X and Y with their time 1 values. In addition to the usual assumptions underlying path analysis employing OLS (Asher, 1976), the model in Figure 6 implies: (1) finite causal lags, i.e., no instantaneous effects in the system—every causal effect exists across a finite time interval; (2) equal lag periods for all causal relationships; (3) the measurement period is less than the time required for a causal effect to occur; and (4) the time between measurements is approximately the same as the causal lag period (Heise, 1970).

Although the cross-lagged correlational method may appear to be straightforward, it can lead to unwarranted inferences under certain conditions, as we shall now see. Given the causal structure in Figure 6, the basic theorem of path analysis (Asher, 1976) implies that $r_{X_1Y_2}$ and $r_{Y_1X_2}$ may be decomposed as:

$$r_{X_1Y_2} = P_1 + r_{X_1Y_1}P_4$$
$$r_{Y_1X_2} = P_2 + r_{X_1Y_1}P_3.$$

[43]

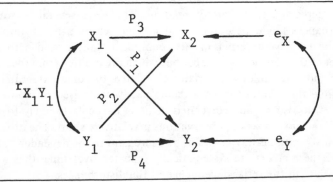

Figure 6: Hypothesized Causal Linkage in a Two-Variable, Two-Wave Model

It can be seen from these equations that the values of the raw cross-lag correlations are affected not only by the magnitudes of the cross-variable causal paths but also by the stabilities of X and Y (P_3 and P_4) and by the simultaneous correlation of the variables ($r_{X_1 Y_1}$). Thus, for example, $r_{Y_1 X_2}$ could be greater than $r_{X_1 Y_2}$ even though $P_2 = 0$, provided the stability of X were markedly larger than the stability of Y.

As in the discussion of regression effects, the conclusion is that a sound analytical strategy necessarily entails controlling for the initial values of the dependent variable(s). In addition, because correlation and standardized regression coefficient values are affected by changes in variances across populations, it will usually be preferable to estimate the parameters of the causal system using unstandardized variables (Blalock, 1967; Kim and Mueller, 1976). A detailed discussion of causal model estimation is beyond the scope of this work. The reader is referred to Asher (1976), Blalock (1971), and Heise (1975).

AUTOCORRELATED DISTURBANCES

To this point it has been assumed that the disturbance in the equation describing the relationship between a dependent variable and one or more regressors is independently distributed over time. There are many situations, however, in which disturbances for each individual may exhibit serial dependence, or *autocorrelation*. There are several reasons why disturbances might be autocorrelated. One reason arises from the fact that the disturbance term is in part a composite of the myriad factors which influence the dependent variable but which are omitted from the analysis. Since most variables are serially correlated to some extent, it is quite probable that the disturbance, being partly comprised of omitted variables, will also be autocorrelated. This is particularly likely to be true if the lag between sets of observations is relatively short. The disturbance term also contains any errors of measurement in the dependent variable, and if these errors are systematically repeated over time, that will also contribute to the serial dependence of the disturbances.

The consequences of autocorrelated disturbances for panel analysis depend on the form of the model being estimated. To take the simpler case first, consider a model in which the current value of Y is posited to be a function of one or more current or lagged values of *other* variables X, Z, and so on. For equations of this sort, OLS will yield unbiased, although inefficient, estimates of the regression coefficients (Johnston, 1972).[14] More important, however, the estimate of V(e), the variance of the disturbance, will be incorrect. In the case of positively autocorrelated disturbances, OLS will underestimate V(e), and hence statistics based on the error variance (R^2, F, the t ratios for the coefficients, and so on) will be inflated.[15] As Hibbs (1973) pointed out, this may result in a spurious attribution of significance to independent variables and seriously impair the empirical process of causal inference.

Usually, one will want to include lagged values of the dependent variable on the right-hand side of the regression equation. Indeed, it is the desire to develop explicitly dynamic models that motivates most panel analysis. Once lagged dependent variables are admitted as regressors, however, OLS no longer yields unbiased estimates of the regression coefficients, and this is true regardless of the sample size. The result is derived mathematically by Johnston (1972), but it may be readily understood from the following example. Consider the equation:

$$Y_2 = \alpha + \beta_1 Y_1 + \beta_2 X_2 + e_2, \qquad [44]$$

which may be diagramed as in Figure 7. The curved arrow indicates the presence of autocorrelated disturbances.

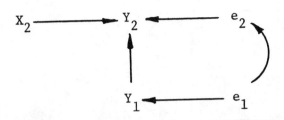

Figure 7: Causal Model of a Simple Dynamic Process with an Autocorrelated Disturbance

Proper application of OLS requires that the disturbance term in Equation 44 be uncorrelated with all regressors. but as can be seen in Figure 7, Y_1 will necessarily be correlated with e_2 via the autocorrelation of the disturbances. The result is that the OLS estimate of the effect of Y_1 on Y_2 will also include the spurious covariance of the Y's due to the disturbance autocorrelation. If the autocorrelation is positive, the OLS estimate of β_1 will be biased upward, and the bias will be downward if the autocorrelation is negative.

The problem parallels the case in which the correlation between two variables, X and Y, is partly due to the effects of a third variable, Z, on both of them, as diagramed in Figure 8. To estimate the effect of X on Y, we must control for the influence of Z, usually via multiple regression or partial correlation. The autocorrelated disturbance in Figure 7 is analogous to the Z variable in that it partly determines the covariance between regressor (Y_1) and dependent variable (Y_2). Correspondingly, what is required is an estimator which "purges" the relationship between Y_1 and Y_2 of the covariation due to the serially dependent disturbance component.

In practice, estimation involves creating a surrogate variable for Y_1 which has the properties of being correlated with Y_1 but uncorrelated with e_2 in Equation 44. If such a surrogate—or *instrumental*—variable can be secured, it may be substituted for Y_1 in Equation 44 as follows. Let $\hat{Y}_1$ be the instrumental variable, so that

$$Y_1 = \hat{Y}_1 + u, \qquad [45]$$

where $\hat{Y}_1$ and u are independently distributed. Then, by substitution into Equation 44,

$$Y_2 = \alpha + \beta_1 \hat{Y}_1 + \beta_2 X_2 + (e_2 + \beta_1 u). \qquad [46]$$

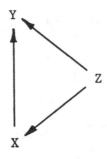

Figure 8: Causal Model with Partly Spurious Relationship between X and Y

By the definition of an instrumental variable, $\hat{Y}_1$ is uncorrelated with the compound disturbance in Equation 46. Further X_2 is uncorrelated with e_2, since the former is an exogenous variable. If the independence of X_2 and u can be assured (see below), then Equation 46 may be consistently estimated by OLS.[16]

The criterion that X_2 and u be independent, as well as the other two criteria of an instrumental variable cited above, is satisfied if $\hat{Y}_1$ is obtained by regressing Y_1 on X_1 and X_2 (Fisher, 1970):

$$Y_1 = \pi_1 + \pi_2 X_1 + \pi_3 X_2 + u. \qquad [47]$$

The X_1 is included as a regressor because it is posited to be related to Y_1 (as is seen by lagging Equation 44 back one time point). The X_2 is also used to form Y_1 so that the independence of X_2 and the compound disturbance in Equation 46 is assured. In general, all exogenous variables appearing in the equation of interest are included in the regression forming the instrumental variable (Johnston, 1972; Fisher, 1970). It might be noted that Equation 47 implies regressing Y_1 on a *subsequent* value of X, which might seem unusual. It is important to bear in mind, however, that the sole purpose of Equation 47 is to secure an instrumental variable possessing certain desired statistical properties. Equation 44 is the structural equation of substantive interest, and Equation 47 represents simply an intermediate step in the estimation procedure. The prediction, $\hat{Y}_1$, obtained from OLS estimation of Equation 47 is then substituted into the original equation, as described by Equation 46. A second application of OLS to Equation 46 yields consistent estimates of the relevant coefficients.[17] Since the complete procedure involves two successive applications of OLS—one to obtain the instrumental variable(s) and one to estimate the equation of interest—the method is referred to as two-stage least squares (2SLS).

EXAMPLE OF A DYNAMIC CAUSAL SYSTEM
WITH AN AUTOCORRELATED DISTURBANCE

Equation 48 posits that citizens' evaluations of former President Nixon in 1976 are dependent on their past evaluations of Nixon (i.e., in 1972) and their party identifications:

$$N_{76} = \alpha + \beta_1 N_{72} + \beta_2 I_{76} + e_{76}. \qquad [48]$$

The data to be used in estimating this equation are derived from the 1972-1976 American Election Panel Study (Converse and Markus, 1979). Evaluations of Nixon are scored on a 0-100 degree "feeling thermometer," and party identification is operationalized by a scale ranging from 1 (Strong Democrat) to 7 (Strong Republican). The assumption is that increasing strength of Republican identification is linked with more favorable evaluations of Nixon.

Because of the possibility of an autocorrelated disturbance, the 2SLS procedure outlined above will be employed as an estimator. The first stage involves regressing N_{72} on I_{72} and I_{76}. The resulting $\hat{N}_{72}$ replaces N_{72} in Equation 48, which is then estimated by a second application of OLS.

The 2SLS estimates of the coefficients in Equation 48 are shown in the left two columns of Table 22. The analysis indicates a fairly strong relationship between current and lagged feelings toward Nixon. In addition, when 1972 feeling scores are taken into account, the influence of current party identification on Nixon evaluations does not attain statistical significance. (The point estimate of the I_{76} coefficient implies about an 8 degree difference, 1.3×6, in the ratings of Nixon by Strong Republicans versus Strong Democrats.)

The discrepancies between the 2SLS and the corresponding OLS estimates (the latter in the right two columns of Table 22) are of the kind one would expect in the presence of a negatively autocorrelated disturbance. The OLS coefficient for the lagged dependent variable is only about 60% of the 2SLS estimate, and the OLS coefficient for I_{76} is correspondingly larger. In this example, a negatively autocorrelated disturbance (and consequent attenuation of the OLS N_{72} coefficient) could well be the result of measurement error in the feeling scores. This possibility leads to the next major topic.

TABLE 22
2SLS and OLS Estimates of the 1976 Nixon Feeling Score Equation

	2SLS		OLS	
	Coefficient	t-ratio	Coefficient	t-ratio
Constant	−18.43	−2.81	−5.76	−2.83
N_{72}	.67	4.87	.40	13.09
I_{76}	1.30	1.50	2.86	7.29
R^2	.22		.23	

Measurement Error

Most variables of interest to social scientists can be measured only imperfectly. Unfortunately, the presence of measurement error poses a serious obstacle for quantitative analysis generally and for studies of change in particular. Consider the following *measurement model* (Blalock, 1968) describing the relationship between observed values, x, true values, X, and measurement errors, ϵ:

$$x = X + \epsilon. \qquad [51]$$

If the true scores and error components in Equation 51 are distributed independently, then the variance of observed scores is simply the sum of the variances of X and ϵ:

$$V(x) = V(X) + V(\epsilon). \qquad [52]$$

The *reliability* of x is defined as the ratio of true score variance to total variance:

$$\rho_{xx}^2 = V(X)/[V(X) + V(\epsilon)]. \qquad [53]$$

Reliability may also be thought of as the squared correlation between observed and true scores (Carmines and Zeller, 1979). In practice, the reliability of a measure is assessed via the correlation of scores on parallel forms of a test, through repeated measurement on the same sample (provided no change in true scores can be assumed a priori), or by more complex modeling procedures.

If a variable has been measured without error on repeated occasions, the difference in an individual's observed scores is true change. But if the measure is unreliable, then $x_2 - x_1$ will be composed of true change plus error:

$$x_2 - x_1 = (X_2 + \epsilon_2) - (X_1 + \epsilon_1)$$
$$= (X_2 - X_1) + (\epsilon_2 - \epsilon_1). \qquad [54]$$

In recent years, methods for separating true change from error have been developed by a number of scholars (Coleman, 1964b; Heise, 1969; Wiley and Wiley, 1970; Wiggins, 1973). Some of these analytical procedures have already been discussed and others will be illustrated in a later section. For the moment, however, I shall focus on some of the consequences of unreliability from a conceptual perspective.

Consider the problem of estimating the relationship between individuals' scores on variable X at two points in time. The true model is:

$$X_2 = \alpha + \beta_1 X_1 + e_2. \qquad [55]$$

But if we possess only imperfect indicators of X, then by substitution of Equation 51 into 55 we have:

$$(x_2 - \epsilon_2) = \alpha + \beta_1(x_1 - \epsilon_1) + e_2$$
$$x_2 = \alpha + \beta_1 x_1 + [(e_2 + \epsilon_2) - \beta_1 \epsilon_1]. \qquad [56]$$

The OLS estimator assumes that the regressor is independent of the disturbance. But this is plainly not true in Equation 56, since the compound disturbance term consists partly of the measurement error contained in x_1.[18] The consequences are not trivial. If we assume that the measurement errors are serially uncorrelated, then it can be shown (Bohrnstedt, 1969) that for large samples.

$$\hat{\beta}_1 = \beta_1 \cdot \rho_{xx}^2. \qquad [57]$$

Since ρ_{xx}^2 is fractional, in the simple case of one regressor the OLS estimate will be biased toward zero by an amount directly proportional to the degree of unreliability in the regressor.[19]

A little reflection on the nature of the problem will show that this result makes sense. We are interested in the relation between true scores X_2 and X_1 but have only imperfect measures whose total variance consists partly of random noise, $V(\epsilon)$. The larger the proportion of total variance that is noise, the smaller the estimated relationship will be, since the co-variation of x_2 with the measurement error in x_1 is zero. In the limiting case, if all of the variation in x_t were random measurement error, then the estimated relationship between x_2 and x_1 would be zero (Hanushek and Jackson, 1977).

WILEY AND WILEY MODEL

Building on earlier work by Heise (1969), Wiley and Wiley (1970) showed that, given certain assumptions, it is possible to use three waves of panel data to estimate the reliability of a measure and the stability of the true values. Consider the model in Figure 9 linking true and observed variables, where x, X, and ϵ are defined as before and e summarizes all exogenous factors which affect the true scores.

The model may be decomposed into two parts: a *causal* model linking the unobserved variables and a *measurement* model associating observed variables to the unobserved constructs. The model in Figure 9 assumes that: (1) the causal model is lag 1, where α_{ji} is the unstandardized regression coefficient linking true scores at times j and i; (2) the exogenous components in the causal model are serially uncorrelated; (3) the measurement model links X_i and x_i in a one-to-one correspondence; and (4) the measurement errors are serially uncorrelated.

As it stands, the model has eight parameters to be estimated from the variance-covariance matrix of observed scores: $V(e_1)$, $V(e_2)$, $V(e_3)$, α_{21}, α_{32}, $V(\epsilon_1)$, $V(\epsilon_2)$, and $V(\epsilon_3)$. However, the observed 3×3 variance-covariance matrix contains only six distinct pieces of information—the variances of x_1, x_2, and x_3, plus the covariances $C(x_1 x_2)$, $C(x_1 x_3)$, and $C(x_2 x_3)$—and therefore a unique solution is not possible unless further assumptions are made. Wiley and Wiley added the assumption of constant error variance, i.e., $V(\epsilon_1) = V(\epsilon_2) = V(\epsilon_3) = V(\epsilon)$. This assumption is a reasonable one for many applied situations, and with it the number of unknowns is reduced to six, thus permitting a unique solution.

The estimating equations are derived as follows. First, Equation Set 58 describes the causal relations among unobserved constructs:

$$X_1 = e_1$$

$$X_2 = \alpha_{21} X_1 + e_2 = \alpha_{21} e_1 + e_2 \qquad [58]$$

$$X_3 = \alpha_{32} X_2 + e_3 = \alpha_{32}(\alpha_{21} e_1 + e_2) + e_3.$$

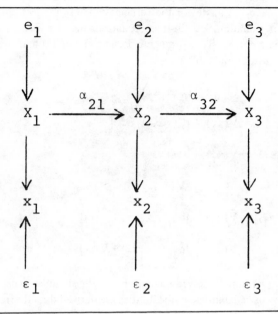

Figure 9: Wiley and Wiley Model

The set of measurement equations is:

$$x_1 = X_1 + \epsilon_1$$
$$x_2 = X_2 + \epsilon_2 \qquad [59]$$
$$x_3 = X_3 + \epsilon_3.$$

By substituting Equations 58 into 59 and taking expected values of the various squares and cross-products, we have:

$$V(x_1) = V(e_1) + V(\epsilon)$$
$$C(x_1 x_2) = \alpha_{21} V(e_1)$$
$$C(x_1 x_3) = \alpha_{21} \alpha_{32} V(e_1)$$
$$V(x_2) = \alpha_{21}^2 V(e_1) + V(e_2) + V(\epsilon) \qquad [60]$$
$$C(x_2 x_3) = \alpha_{32} [\alpha_{21}^2 V(e_1) + V(e_2)]$$
$$V(x_3) = \alpha_{32}^2 [\alpha_{21}^2 V(e_1) + V(e_2)] + V(e_3) + V(\epsilon).$$

When observed estimates of the variances and covariances replace the left-hand side of Equation Set 60, these equations may be used to estimate the unknown parameters. By rearranging Equation Set 60 and making appropriate substitutions, one obtains:

$$\hat{\alpha}_{32} = \hat{C}(x_1 x_3) / \hat{C}(x_1 x_2)$$

$$\hat{V}(\epsilon) = \hat{V}(x_2) - [\hat{C}(x_2 x_3) / \hat{\alpha}_{32}]$$

$$\hat{V}(e_1) = \hat{V}(x_1) - \hat{V}(\epsilon)$$

$$\hat{\alpha}_{21} = \hat{C}(x_1 x_2) / \hat{V}(e_1)$$

$$\hat{V}(e_2) = \hat{V}(x_2) - [\hat{\alpha}_{21} \hat{C}(x_1 x_2) + \hat{V}(\epsilon)]$$

$$\hat{V}(e_3) = \hat{V}(x_3) - [\hat{\alpha}_{32} \hat{C}(x_2 x_3) + \hat{V}(\epsilon)] .$$

[61]

Equation Set 61 may be solved recursively for the six unknowns.

Estimates of reliabilities and stabilities are derived directly from the above solutions. By Equations 53 and 58:

$$\rho_{11}^2 = \frac{V(X_1)}{V(X_1) + V(\epsilon)} = \frac{V(e_1)}{V(e_1) + V(\epsilon)}$$

$$\rho_{22}^2 = \frac{V(X_2)}{V(X_2) + V(\epsilon)} = \frac{\alpha_{21}^2 V(e_1) + V(e_2)}{\alpha_{21}^2 V(e_1) + V(e_2) + V(\epsilon)}$$

[62]

$$\rho_{33}^2 = \frac{V(X_3)}{V(X_3) + V(\epsilon)} = \frac{\alpha_{32}^2 [\alpha_{21}^2 V(e_1) + V(e_2)] + V(e_3)}{\alpha_{32}^2 [\alpha_{21}^2 V(e_1) + V(e_2)] + V(e_3) + V(\epsilon)} .$$

The stability coefficients, γ_{ij}, are defined as the correlations between the true scores at times i and j. They are obtained by standardizing the α_{ij} as follows:

$$\gamma_{12} = \alpha_{21} \sqrt{V(X_1)} / \sqrt{V(X_2)}$$

$$\gamma_{23} = \alpha_{32} \sqrt{V(X_2)} / \sqrt{V(X_3)}$$

[63]

$$\gamma_{13} = \alpha_{21} \, \alpha_{32} \, \sqrt{V(X_1)} \, / \, \sqrt{V(X_3)}.$$

An application of the Wiley-Wiley approach. Table 23 shows the variance-covariance matrix for the seven-step party identification measure as obtained from the 1972-1974-1976 American Election Panel (N = 1,237). Substitution of these values into Equation 61 yields the following estimates:

$$\hat{\alpha}_{32} \quad = .9704$$

$$\hat{V}(\epsilon) \quad = .6763$$

$$\hat{V}(e_1) = 3.4527$$

$$\hat{\alpha}_{21} \quad = .9672$$

$$\hat{V}(e_2) = .2390$$

$$\hat{V}(e_3) = .1374.$$

Based on these values, the estimated stability and reliability coefficients using Equations 62 and 63 are:

$$\hat{\rho}_{11}^2 = .836 \qquad\qquad \hat{\gamma}_{12} = .965$$

$$\hat{\rho}_{22}^2 = .837 \qquad\qquad \hat{\gamma}_{23} = .980$$

$$\hat{\rho}_{33}^2 = .834 \qquad\qquad \hat{\gamma}_{13} = .945.$$

These results suggest that the reliability of the party identification measure is fairly constant over time and that true party identification is quite stable from one election to the next. By comparing the $\hat{\gamma}_{ij}$ values with the observed stability correlations in Table 23, the downward bias due to measurement error is apparent.

THE LISREL MODEL

Recently, a number of researchers have developed techniques for estimating the parameters of causal models in the presence of measurement error. These methods may be seen as generalizations of the Wiley-

TABLE 23
United States Party Identification Variance-Covariance Matrix

	1972	1974	1976
1972	4.1290		
1974	3.3395 (.807)	4.1453	
1976	3.2406 (.790)	3.3663 (.819)	4,0804

Note: Correlations are in parentheses.

Wiley approach in that the question posed is: Given a particular causal model and measurement model, is it possible to estimate consistently the relevant parameters of the system from the observed variance-covariance matrix? Joreskog and others (Joreskog, 1973; Joreskog and Sorbom, 1976; Werts et al., 1971) have devised a maximum-likelihood procedure which will estimate the parameters for a wide range of causal/measurement models, provided such models are identified (i.e., there are at least as many unique observed variance-covariance values as there are parameters to be estimated). A detailed discussion of the procedure—called LISREL for LInear Structural RELations—is beyond the scope of the present work. Nevertheless, LISREL is becoming increasingly useful in panel analysis (Wheaton et al., 1977; Kohn and Schooler, 1978; Wheaton, 1978), and it is important for the panel researcher to grasp a basic overview of the approach and its application.

As in the Wiley-Wiley method, a distinction is made between the causal model, which describes relationships between exogenous and endogenous unobserved constructs, and the measurement model, which links the unobserved constructs to the measured variables. The parameters of the entire system may be grouped into eight matrices:

Λ_y: a matrix of coefficients linking observed measures to endogenous constructs

Λ_x: a similar matrix linking observed measures to exogenous constructs

B: the coefficient matrix for the endogenous constructs

Γ: the coefficient matrix linking exogenous to endogenous constructs

Ψ: the variance-covariance matrix for the stochastic disturbances in the causal model

θ_ϵ: the variance-covariance matrix for the measurement errors of the observed endogenous measures

θ_δ: a similar variance-covariance matrix for the measurement errors of the observed exogenous measures

Φ: the variance-covariance matrix for the exogenous constructs.

The matrices **B**, **Γ**, **Ψ**, and **Φ** refer to the causal model of unobserved constructs. **B** and **Γ** are matrices of regression coefficients, while **Ψ** and **Φ** are variance-covariance matrices for the disturbances and exogenous constructs, respectively. The matrices Λ_y, Λ_x, θ_ϵ, and θ_δ refer to the measurement model. The first links observed measures to their endogenous unobserved counterparts (i.e., the dependent variables in the causal model), while the second links measures to the unobserved exogenous, or independent, variables. Finally, θ_ϵ and θ_δ are variance-covariance matrices for the measurement errors associated with endogenous and exogenous measures, respectively.

If we let X, Y be the unmeasured constructs and x, y be the measured variables, then in matrix notation the causal model is:

$$
\begin{array}{ccccc}
\text{BY} & = & \Gamma\text{X} & + & \text{e} \\
(m \times m)\,(m \times 1) & & (m \times n)\,(n \times 1) & & (m \times 1),
\end{array} \qquad [64]
$$

where there are m endogenous and n exogenous constructs. This model is identical to systems of simultaneous equations typically studied by econometricians (Kmenta, 1971).

The measurement model is:

$$
\begin{array}{cccccc}
y & = & \Lambda_y\,Y & + & \epsilon \\
(p \times 1) & & (p \times m)\,(m \times 1) & & (p \times 1) \\[2mm]
x & = & \Lambda_x\,X & + & \delta \\
(q \times 1) & & (q \times n)\,(q \times 1) & & (q \times 1)
\end{array} \qquad [65]
$$

There are p observed measures of the endogenous constructs and q observed measures of exogenous constructs. Measurement models recall the conceptual structures that are the focus of factor-analytic research by psychometricians (Hauser and Goldberger, 1971).

Since the LISREL method places few restrictions on the sorts of causal and measurement models that may be postulated (within the bounds of identifiability), it is a flexible and powerful tool for the analysis of panel and other kinds of data. The problem, as with any kind of analysis, is for the researcher to provide a well-specified theoretical model to be evaluated.

A LISREL application. To provide a simple empirical example of a LISREL application to panel data, I have merged a model of candidate preference with a model of measurement error in the party identification variable, resulting in the hypothesized system which appears in Figure 10.

62

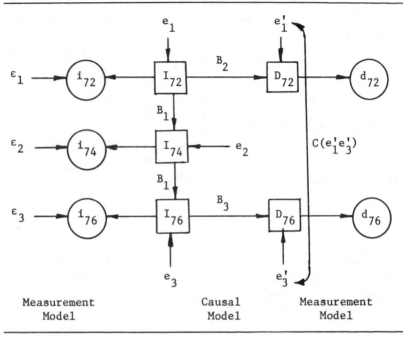

Figure 10: Hypothesized LISREL Model (Variables in squares are unobserved constructs; variables in circles are observed measures. Paths without coefficients have implicit coefficients of 1.0. Primes on the disturbances in the causal model distinguish disturbances for I_t from those for D_t.)

The measurement model for party identification is identical to the model used in the Wiley-Wiley example (Figure 9), with the exception that the coefficients for the two causal paths $I_{72} \rightarrow I_{74}$ and $I_{74} \rightarrow I_{76}$ are constrained to be equal. For expository purposes, the causal model posits linkages between contemporaneous identification, I_t, and a candidate preference differential, D_t. The latter concept is measured by the difference between the feeling thermometer scores assigned to the Republican and Democratic presidential candidates at time t. The model assumes that the preference differentials are measured without error. Last, the stochastic factors affecting D_t are permitted to be autocorrelated.

The model contains no exogenous variables (I_{72} is treated as lagged endogenous), so there are no Γ, Φ, Λ_x, or θ_δ matrices to specify. The B, Λ_y, Ψ, and θ_ϵ matrices are:

$$
B = \begin{bmatrix}
1 & 0 & 0 & 0 & 0 \\
-B_1 & 1 & 0 & 0 & 0 \\
0 & -B_1 & 1 & 0 & 0 \\
-B_2 & 0 & 0 & 1 & 0 \\
0 & 0 & -B_3 & 0 & 1
\end{bmatrix}
$$

$$
\Lambda_y = \begin{bmatrix}
1 & 0 & 0 & 0 & 0 \\
0 & 1 & 0 & 0 & 0 \\
0 & 0 & 1 & 0 & 0 \\
0 & 0 & 0 & 1 & 0 \\
0 & 0 & 0 & 0 & 1
\end{bmatrix}
$$

$$
\Psi = \begin{bmatrix}
V(e_1) & 0 & 0 & 0 & 0 \\
0 & V(e_2) & 0 & 0 & 0 \\
0 & 0 & V(e_3) & 0 & 0 \\
0 & 0 & 0 & V(e_1') & C(e_1' e_3') \\
0 & 0 & 0 & C(e_3' e_1') & V(e_3')
\end{bmatrix}
$$

$$
\Theta_\epsilon = \begin{bmatrix}
V(\epsilon) & 0 & 0 & 0 & 0 \\
0 & V(\epsilon) & 0 & 0 & 0 \\
0 & 0 & V(\epsilon) & 0 & 0 \\
0 & 0 & 0 & 0 & 0 \\
0 & 0 & 0 & 0 & 0
\end{bmatrix}
$$

Once preliminary estimates of the relevant parameters are provided by the analyst, the LISREL estimation program calculates maximum-likelihood estimates and standard errors via an iterative procedure using the observed variance-covariance matrix as input. Additional output from the program is useful for diagnosing model specification errors and evaluating the overall goodness of fit of the hypothesized model to the observed data (see Joreskog and Sorbom, 1976; Sorbom, 1975).

The maximum-likelihood estimates of the parameters for the model in Figure 10 are presented in Table 24. The estimated values are all many times larger than their associated standard errors, indicating that all parameters are significantly different from zero. The estimated B values are consistent with those derived from the previous examples employing these data. These generally positive results are somewhat mitigated by the fairly high χ^2 value, suggesting a lack of fit for the model. Additional diagnostic output (not shown here) points to the assumption of error-free d_t measures and/or independence between e_i and e_i' as possible sources of the lack of fit (see Sorbom, 1975). Exclusive reliance on the χ^2 test must be tempered by substantive considerations, however, since, as Sorbom put it, "when the number of observations is large, the χ^2 values may well indicate that any conceptually plausible model is nonacceptable" (1975: 144).

The purpose of this example was not to present a complete and validated model of partisan behavior. Rather, it was to suggest the type of problem for which the technique is appropriate and to illustrate how it is applied. The literature on LISREL modeling is growing quickly, and the interested researcher is urged to consult it for a more complete treatment (Long, 1976).

4. CONCLUDING NOTE

In this paper, I have presented a variety of methods for the analysis of panel data. Each technique is derived from a set of assumptions, and it is important for the researcher to bear in mind that the results of any analysis are only as good as the correspondence between these assumptions and the properties of the empirical system under study. Analytical techniques, no matter how elegant or powerful, will only generate nonsense when applied inappropriately.

It is worth mentioning in closing that a number of topics in the analysis of panel data have necessarily been overlooked here, either because of their technical complexity or because they are only beginning to be ex-

TABLE 24
LISREL Estimates of Model Parameters

Parameter	Unstandardized Estimate	Standard Error	Standardized Estimate
B_1	.94	.01	.95
B_2	13.66	.73	.56
B_3	11.82	.59	.59
$V(e_1)$	3.69	.20	1.00
$V(e_2)$	.39	.07	.11
$V(e_3)$	.37	.07	.10
$V(e_1')$	1530.05	74.47	.69
$V(e_3')$	954.95	46.81	.66
$C(e_1' e_3')$	314.77	43.06	.18
$V(\epsilon)$	.53	.04	.53

$\chi^2 = 39.31$ df = 5

plored by social scientists. One such topic involves the use of continuous time processes, as opposed to the discrete time techniques presented here. The interested reader is referred to Coleman (1964a), Spilerman (1972), and Singer and Spilerman (1974) for an introduction. A second important topic is derived from the consideration of panel data as a pooling of a large number of short time series—one for each respondent, nation, or such. A recent piece by Hannan and Young (1977) is a good beginning for an exploration of that analytical perspective.

NOTES

1. Readers not familiar with matrix operations may wish to consult one of the many good introductions to linear algebra, such as Bashaw (1969).

2. The time intervals between the waves are not so disparate as the yearly dates suggest. The span between successive surveys was about 17 months.

3. The t subscript is necessary for the R(t) matrix because the transition probabilities are dependent on the time lapse.

4. For those not familiar with calculus, the idea behind Equation 16 can be described as follows: at time t take the proportion of individuals at each point v_{it} on the 0-1 attitude continuum, $f(v_{it})$, and multiply this proportion by the corresponding probability (density) of giving response i, v_{it}. The (infinite) sum of these products yields P_{it}.

5. The Goodman approach may be extended to include polytomous dependent and independent variables, but for expository simplicity I consider only binary variables.

6. In multivariate contingency table analysis in which no distinction is made between independent and dependent variables, the terms *main effects* and *interaction effects* are not interpreted quite the same way as they are in the usual ANOVA (Davis, 1974); in the context being described in this paper, however, the interpretations are consistent with ANOVA.

7. "Homoscedastic" refers to the OLS assumption that the variance of the disturbance distribution is constant for all observations. "Inefficiency" refers to the idea that the sampling distribution of the OLS estimator has a larger variance than that of an alternative estimator, weighted least squares. A caret or "hat" over a parameter indicates a sample estimate.

8. The coefficients for an unsaturated model are calculated from the set of frequencies that would be expected under the model, as generated by an iterative maximum-likelihood procedure (Goodman, 1972b; Davis, 1974).

9. Using the notation that V( ) means "variance of . . ." and C( ) means "covariance of . . . ," the correlation between change score and initial value is:

$$\rho_{Y_2-Y_1 \cdot Y_1} = \frac{C[(Y_2 - Y_1)Y_1]}{[V(Y_2 - Y_1) \, V(Y_1)]^{1/2}}$$

$$= \frac{C(Y_2, Y_1) - V(Y_1)}{[V(Y_2 - Y_1) \, V(Y_1)]^{1/2}} \, .$$

By definition, the covariance of two variables can never be greater than the square root of the product of their variances (consider the formula for a correlation coefficient). Therefore, if we assume the system is in equilibrium, so that $V(Y_2) = V(Y_1)$, then,

$$C(Y_2, Y_1) < [V(Y_2) \, V(Y_1)]^{1/2} = V(Y_1),$$

unless the correlation between Y_2 and Y_1 is perfect. Hence, the numerator of the formula for $\rho_{Y_2-Y_1 \cdot Y_1}$ will be negative.

10. Once the possibility of measurement error is introduced, the distinction between true change and response error becomes meaningful. This will be discussed shortly.

11. Experimental researchers may prefer analysis of covariance. This can be shown to be equivalent to a multiple regression approach (Johnston, 1972).

12. For further discussion of dummy variables in regression analysis, see Johnston (1972) or Hanushek and Jackson (1977).

13. The assumptions underlying the OLS estimator are: (1) the model to be estimated is correctly specified; (2) the independent variables are measured without error, and the values they take on have either been fixed, as in an experiment, or else are stochastic with distributions that are independent of the disturbances; and (3) the disturbances are independently distributed and are sampled from a distribution having a mean of zero and a constant variance. Much of the remainder of this paper will elaborate upon situations in which one or more of these assumptions are not satisfied.

14. "Unbiased" means that the expected value of the estimate is the true population parameter value. Efficiency is defined in Note 7.

15. These results are based on the assumption that one or more of the independent variables is itself serially correlated. Should the independent variables be approximately randomly distributed over time, then the bias in the estimate of $V(e)$ is not likely to be serious (Johnston, 1972).

16. An estimator is consistent if its bias (if any) decreases to zero as the sample size increases.

17. The standard errors and ANOVA obtained from this regression are not appropriate for testing the significance of the coefficients in Equation 44. Instead, the coefficient estimates from Equation 46 should be used in conjunction with the *original* variables (as opposed to the instruments) to calculate the estimated error variance and, thereby, the estimated standard errors (see Johnston, 1972). The two-stage least-squares programs in commonly employed statistical packages (e.g., SPSS, OSIRIS, and such) automatically make this adjustment and print out the appropriate estimates.

18. Note that so long as measurement errors are serially independent, the measurement error in x_2 does not affect the OLS estimates of the coefficients in Equation 56.

19. The downward bias will occur as a necessity only in the case of one regressor; in the multivariate case, the situation is more complex, but generally OLS is inconsistent (Johnston, 1972).

REFERENCES

ANDERSON, T. W. (1954) "Probability models for analyzing time changes in attitudes," in P. F. Lazarsfeld (ed.), Mathematical Thinking in the Social Sciences. New York: Macmillian.

ASHER, H. B. (1976) "Causal Modeling." Sage University Paper series on Quantitative Applications in the Social Sciences, 07-003. Beverly Hills, CA: Sage.

BASHAW, W. L. (1969) Mathematics for Statistics. New York: John Wiley.

BECK, P. A. (1975) "Models for analyzing panel data: a comparative review." Political Methodology 2: 357-380.

BISHOP, Y.M.M., S. E. FIENBERG, and P. W. HOLLAND (1975) Discrete Multivariate Analysis. Cambridge: MIT Press.

BLALOCK, H. M., Jr. (1971) Causal Models in the Social Sciences. Chicago: AVC.

——— (1970) "Estimating measurement error using multiple indicators and several points in time." American Sociological Review 35: 101-111.

——— (1968) "The measurement problem: a gap between the language of theory and research," in H. M. Blalock, Jr. and A. B. Blalock (eds.), Methodology in Social Research. New York: McGraw-Hill.

——— (1967) "Causal inferences, closed populations, and measures of association." American Political Science Review 61: 130-136.

BLUMEN, I., M. KOGAN, and P. J. McCARTHY (1955) The Industrial Mobility of Labor as a Probability Process. Ithaca, NY: Cornell University Press.

BOHRNSTEDT, G. W. (1969) "Observations on the measurement of change," in E. F. Borgotta (ed.), Sociological Methodology 1969. San Francisco: Jossey-Bass.

BUTLER, D. and D. STOKES (1969) Political Change in Britain. New York: St. Martin's Press.

CAMPBELL, D. T. (1963) "From description to experimentation: interpreting trends as quasi-experiments," in C. W. Harris (ed.), Problems in Measuring Change. Madison: University of Wisconsin Press.

——— and K. N. CLAYTON (1961) "Avoiding regression effects in panel studies of communication impact." (unpublished)

CAMPBELL, D. T. and J. C. STANLEY (1963) Experimental and Quasi-Experimental Designs for Research. Chicago: Rand McNally.

CARMINES, E. G. and R. A. ZELLER (1979) "Reliability and Validity Assessment." Sage University Paper series on Quantitative Applications in the Social Sciences, 07-017. Beverly Hills, CA: Sage.

COLEMAN, J. S. (1964a) Introduction to Mathematical Sociology. New York: Macmillan.

——— (1964b) Models of Change and Response Uncertainty. Englewood Cliffs, NJ: Prentice-Hall.

CONVERSE, P. E. (1970) "Attitudes and non-attitudes: continuation of a dialogue," in E. R. Tufte (ed.), The Quantitative Analysis of Social Problems. Reading, MA: Addison-Wesley.

——— (1969) "Of time and partisan stability." Comparative Political Studies 2: 139-171.

——— (1964) "The nature of belief systems in mass publics," in D. E. Apter (ed.), Ideology and Discontent. New York: Macmillan.

——— and G. B. MARKUS (1979) "Plus ca change . . . : the new CPS election study panel." American Political Science Review 73: 32-49.

CRONBACH, L. J. and L. FURBY (1970) "How we should measure "change"—or should we?" Psychological Bulletin 74: 68-80.

DAVIS, J. A. (1974) "Hierarchical models for significance testing in multivariate contingency tables," in H. L. Costner (ed.), Sociological Methodology 1973-1974. San Francisco: Jossey-Bass.

70

DUNCAN, O. D. (1972) "Unmeasured variables in linear models for panel analysis," in H. L. Costner (ed.), Sociological Methodology 1972. San Francisco: Jossey-Bass.

FISHER, F. M. (1970) "Simultaneous equations estimation: the state of the art." (unpublished)

GILLESPIE, M. W. (1977) "Log-linear techniques and the regression analysis of dummy dependent variables: further bases for comparison." Sociological Methods and Research 6: 103-122.

GOODMAN, L. A. (1976) "The relationship between modified and usual multiple regression approaches to the analysis of the dichotomous variables," in D. R. Heise (ed.), Sociological Methodology 1976. San Francisco: Jossey-Bass.

—— (1973) "Causal analysis of data from panel studies and other surveys. American Journal of Sociology 78: 1135-1191.

—— (1972a) "A general model for the analysis of surveys." American Journal of Sociology 77: 1035-1086.

—— (1972b) "A modified multiple regression approach to the analysis of dichotomous variables." American Sociological Review 37: 28-46.

—— (1970) "The multivariate analysis of qualitative data. Journal of the American Statistical Association 65: 226-256.

—— (1962) "Statistical methods for analyzing processes of change." American Journal of Sociology 68: 57-78.

—— (1961) "Statistical methods for the mover-stayer model." Journal of the American Statistical Association 56: 841-868.

GRIZZLE, J. E., C. R. STARMER, and G. G. KOCH (1969) "Analysis of categorical data by linear models." Biometrics 25: 489-504.

HANNAN, M. T. and A. A. YOUNG (1977) "Estimation in panel models: results on pooling cross sections and time series," in D. R. Heise (ed.), Sociological Methodology 1977. San Francisco: Jossey-Bass.

HANUSHEK, E. A. and J. E. JACKSON (1977) Statistical Methods for Social Scientists. New York: Academic Press.

HAUSER, R. M. and A. S. GOLDBERGER (1971) "The treatment of unobservable variables in path analysis," in H. L. Costner (ed.), Sociological Methodology 1971. San Francisco: Jossey-Bass.

HAYS, W. L. (1973) Statistics for the Social Sciences. New York: Holt, Rinehart and Winston.

HEISE, D. R. (1975) Causal Analysis. New York: John Wiley.

—— (1970) "Causal inference from panel data," in E. F. Borgotta and G. W. Bohrnstedt (eds.), Sociological Methodology 1970. San Francisco: Jossey-Bass.

—— (1969) "Separating reliability and stability in test-retest correlation." American Sociological Review 34: 93-101.

HIBBS, D. A., Jr. (1973) Mass Political Violence. New York: John Wiley.

HYMAN, H. H. (1972) Secondary Analysis of Sample Surveys. New York: John Wiley.

IVERSEN, G. R. and H. NORPOTH (1976) "Analysis of Variance." Sage University Paper series on Quantitative Applications in the Social Sciences, 07-001. Beverly Hills, CA: Sage.

JENNINGS, M. K. and G. B. MARKUS (1977) "The effects of military service on political attitudes: a panel study." American Political Science Review 71: 131-147.

JOHNSTON, J. (1972) Econometric Methods. New York: McGraw-Hill.

JORESKOG, K. G. (1973) A general method for estimating a linear structural equation system," in A. S. Goldberger and O. D. Duncan (eds.), Structural Equation Models in the Social Sciences. New York: Seminar.

—— and D. SORBOM (1976) LISREL—Estimation of Linear Structural Equation Systems by Maximum Likelihood Methods. Chicago: International Educational Services.

KEMENY, J. G., L. SNELL, and G. L. THOMPSON (1966) Finite Mathematics. Englewood Cliffs, NJ: Prentice-Hall.

KIM, J. and C. W. MUELLER (1976) "Standardized and unstandardized coefficients in causal analysis: an expository note." Sociological Methods and Research 4: 423-438.

KISH, L. (1965) Survey Sampling. New York: John Wiley.

KMENTA, J. (1971) Elements of Econometrics. New York: Macmillan.

KOHN, M. L. and C. SCHOOLER (1978) "The reciprocal effects of the substantive complexity of work and intellectual flexibility: a longitudinal assessment." American Journal of Sociology 84: 24-52.

LAZARSFELD, P. F. (1950) "The interpretation and computation of latent structures," in S. A. Stouffer et al. (eds.), Measurement and Prediction (vol. 4 of Studies in Social Psychology in World War II). Princeton, NJ: Princeton University Press.

LONG, J. S. (1976) "Estimation and hypothesis testing in linear models containing measurement error: a review of Joreskog's model for the analysis of covariance structures. Sociological Methods and Research 5: 157-206.

LORD, F. M. (1963) "Elementary models for measuring change," in C. W. Harris (ed.), Problems in Measuring Change. Madison: University of Wisconsin Press.

OSTROM, C. W., Jr. (1978) "Time Series Analysis: Regression Techniques." Sage University Paper series on Quantitative Applications in the Social Sciences, 07-009. Beverly Hills, CA: Sage.

REYNOLDS, H. T. (1977) "Analysis of Nominal Data." Sage University Paper series on Quantitative Applications in the Social Sciences, 07-007. Beverly Hills, CA: Sage.

ROZELLE, R. M. and D. T. CAMPBELL (1969) "More plausible rival hypotheses in the cross-lagged panel correlation technique." Psychological Bulletin 71: 74-80.

SHINGLES, R. (1976) "Causal inference in cross-lagged panel analysis." Political Methodology 3: 95-133.

SINGER, B. and S. SPILERMAN (1974) "Social mobility models for heterogeneous populations," in H. L. Costner (ed.), Sociological Methodology 1973-1974. San Francisco: Jossey-Bass.

SORBOM, D. (1975) "Detection of correlated errors in longitudinal data." British Journal of Mathematical and Statistical Psychology 28: 138-151.

SPILERMAN, S. (1972) "Extensions of the mover-stayer model." American Journal of Sociology 78: 599-627.

TAYLOR, C. L. and M. T. HUDSON [eds.] (1972) World Handbook of Political and Social Indicators. New Haven, CT: Yale University Press.

THORNDIKE, E. L. (1924) "The influence of chance imperfections of measures upon the relationship of initial score to gain or loss. Journal of Experimental Psychology 7: 225-232.

WERTS, E. E., R. L. LINN, and K. G. JORESKOG (1971) "Estimating the parameters of path models involving unmeasured variables," in H. M. Blalock, Jr. (ed.) Causal Models in the Social Sciences. Chicago: AVC.

WHEATON, B. (1978) "The sociogenesis of psychological disorder: reexamining the causal issues with longitudinal data." American Sociological Review 43: 383-403.

——— B. MUTHEN, D. F. ALWIN, and G. F. SUMMERS (1977) "Assessing reliability and stability in panel models," in D. R. Heise (ed.), Sociological Methodology 1977. San Francisco: Jossey-Bass.

WIGGINS, L. M. (1973) Panel Analysis. San Francisco: Jossey-Bass.

WILEY, D. E. and J. A. WILEY (1970) "The estimation of measurement error in panel data." American Sociological Review 35: 112-117.

YEE, A. H. and N. L. GAGE (1968) "Techniques for estimating the source and direction of causal influence in panel data." Psychological Bulletin 70: 115-126.

GREGORY B. MARKUS is Assistant Professor of Political Science and Assistant Research Scientist at the Center for Political Studies, University of Michigan, from where he received his Ph.D. in 1975. His primary research interest is the modeling of sociopolitical attitudes and behavior.

Quantitative Applications
in the Social Sciences

(a Sage University Papers Series)

$6.50 each

Place
Stamp
here

SAGE PUBLICATIONS, INC.

P.O. BOX 5084

NEWBURY PARK, CALIFORNIA 91359–9924